MW01036568

"With classic films and loves that tran
we love and love to hate and/or wish
present-of-choice for weddings, anni
Valentine's Day!"

—Reece Michaelson, writer, editor, researcher, and voracious rom-com watcher

"I will give this book to couples I know who can learn from it and be
inspired by it. The author's words remind me what romantic stories are
all about."

—Pam Wallace, cowriter of Academy Award–winning screenplay *Witness*

"*Romantic Comedies* takes the movies I love and tells me why I love them.
Analyzing the reasons the stories—and relationships—work is fascinating,
and gives me great insight on my own writing. I highly recommend it for
everyone—but especially for writers who write about love."

—Jeannie Eddy, writer/editor, screenwriter, former workshop scheduler for
Romance Writers of America's Kiss of Death chapter

"After reading Pamela Jaye Smith's *Romantic Comedies*, I will no
longer be watching rom-coms with a cheesecake, in tears, just after a
relationship ends. I am going to watch them with my girlfriend, while
we are still together, to prevent that from ever happening."

—Scott Perlman, writer/director

"If you want to spice up your romantic life, delve into *Romantic
Comedies*. Pamela is a story expert, and she has now presented the
mythology of love in a new and creative way, analyzing the types
of love stories in films, so that you can better understand your own
mythic journey and love life."

—Jen Waters, Pen Jen's Songs, Inkwell, & Productions (including a Grammy
nomination)

"I am usually not a rom-com fan, but reading this book makes me want
to watch more of them."

—Sally Shepard, award-winning producer, screenwriter, actress, filmmaker

"Loved *Romantic Comedies* and the opportunity it gave me to
reminisce about all the great rom-coms I've seen over the years. Watch
these films, read this book, and you will be an expert on love."

—Steven Finly, novelist, screenwriter

"By culling wisdom, philosophy, and in-depth ideas from a body of
cinematic stories, the author has written a must-read tome for anyone
interested in becoming a better lover and beloved. This brings a whole
new level of meaning to the movie date night!"

—Kate McCallum, producer; founder, c3: Center for Conscious Creativity

"For anyone who has loved and lost or is afraid to love or is happily in love, Pamela Jaye Smith's book gives us a structural and armchair therapist breakdown of the problems, pitfalls, and solutions of falling in love using some of our favorite romantic comedies."
—Kathie Fong Yoneda, hopeless romantic and author of *The Script-Selling Game*

"This fun and easy reference guide shows all the different ways of love— some that I have never even thought of before!"
—Deborah J. Richardson, rom-com enthusiast

"Not just for the hopeless romantics... a fun journey of self-discovery, while also being an entertaining guide to both new and classic love stories. A great guide for date nights or a coffee table conversation piece, it has something to offer movie buffs as well as those looking for a little more from this genre."
—Cathy Schmalfuss, writer, producer, director

"Being such a movie buff, I've probably seen almost all the films, but what a wonderful reminder of which ones to see again, to order on Netflix."
—Martina Lewis, educator and long-time film buff

"Somewhere between romantic self-help and laughing delight, this book is a romantic comedy Rosetta Stone, elevating 'chick flicks' to relationship definers. As affordable relationship therapy, it provides a roadmap for a laugh-filled, sublimely precarious trip on the celluloid highway of love."
—Gail Jorden, artist, retired production designer, tiny home enthusiast

"*Romantic Comedies* dances in the psyche and serenades the soul. When used in proper context, it will lead lost hearts from chasing due north to centering on *true* north."
—Miquiel Banks, award-winning editor and technical writer, author of *Angels in the Desert*

"This book will make you smile remembering your favorite characters and scenes, introduce you to some movies you haven't seen (and will want to), and most importantly, it will inspire you to consider your own attitudes and behavior when it comes to love."
—Lindsay Smith, entrepreneur, writer-producer, artist

"This book could be used as a guide to finding just the right movie to help find true love or to heal a broken heart."
—Carolyn Handler Miller, screenwriter and author of *Digital Storytelling: A Creator's Guide to Interactive Storytelling*

Pamela Jaye Smith

ROMANTIC COMEDIES

These **FILMS**
Can Save Your
Love Life!

MICHAEL WIESE PRODUCTIONS

Published by Michael Wiese Productions
12400 Ventura Blvd. #1111
Studio City, CA 91604
(818) 379-8799, (818) 986-3408 (FAX)
mw@mwp.com
www.mwp.com

Cover design by Johnny Ink. www.johnnyink.com
Interior design by William Morosi
Copyediting by Gary Sunshine
Printed by SC (Sang Choy) International Pte Ltd

Manufactured in China

To all those wonderful tellers of magical, memorable love stories — from the earliest myths to tomorrow's hit media

Acknowledgments

Thanks to Ken Lee and Michael Wiese of Michael Wiese Productions for the invitation and opportunity to write this book. It's always a pleasure to work with such a professional creative publishing team, including Bill Morosi, who has done such amazing design work for this book, copy editor Gary Sunshine, and cover designer John Brenner.

A world of thanks to the very talented and creative Sherry Garrett, whose generous insights and thoughtful input have made writing this book ever so much more fun. And to Geralyn "Bee" and Ted Rutherford for their gracious assistance in making that possible.

Many thanks to those who at various points in the creative process offered suggestions and feedback: Monty Hayes McMillan, Kathie Fong Yoneda, Steve Finly, Geffrey von Gerlach, Aurora Miller, Pam Wallace, Linda Seger, Cathy Schmalfuss, Jill Gurr, Sally Shepard, Reece Michaelson, Gail Jorden, Pam Shepard, Laural Hardin Smith, Janet Smith, and Debbie Richardson.

For loaning me rom-com movies from their libraries: Kathie Fong Yoneda, Aurora Miller, and Sally Shepard. Thanks for all the tech expertise in pulling images from the films goes to Sally Shepard, Mike Restaino, and Brian Dyer.

Conversations over the years about love and romance have also influenced this book. For that I give thanks to Monty Hayes McMillan, Michael Wilson Woods, Rick Gilligan, Bruce Logan, Geffrey von Gerlach, Sherry Garrett, Thomas Dempsey, Jim Bogard, Paula Lewis, Lori Imbler Vernon, Karen Cozart, Judith Claire, Brian Dyer, Bob Reed, Denise Daniels Fanning, Starrs McBurney, Milton Allen, Adrian Day, Gary Durney, and more. I also learned much about the dynamics of love and relationships from Dave Kaplowitz, Licensed Marriage and Family Therapist and Certified Group Psychotherapist.

Contents

SECTION ONE

SECTION TWO

SECTION THREE

SECTION FOUR

SECTION FIVE

Introduction

Ah, love — one of the strongest forces in the universe. How do you feel about it?

You're in love. You want to be in love. You used to be in love. You're still in love, but they're not. Your love is gone.

Emotions run the gamut in these different states and sometimes you just need a bit of understanding or cheering up, some hopefulness. Sometimes you need some advice on how to handle a situation. And sometimes, what you really need is just a good cry.

Or say one of you wants more communication, sex, intimacy, and/or commitment than the other one does. There's no way you'd get them into couples therapy, so how do you get your point across in an entertaining, thoughtful, and hopefully effective way?

Watch a romantic comedy!

Studies suggest that couples who watch romantic movies together and then discuss them and their feelings about them may have a better stay-together rate than similar couples who enter traditional therapy. Why would that be?

Science has shown us how endorphins work, how the imagination triggers endorphins, how mirror neurons help us experience what we see other people going through, and how the memories of an imagined event or a movie are as real as memories of actual events. It's how stories work.

It's why romantic comedies have been popular for as long as humans have been telling stories: from tales around a campfire; to comedies in an amphitheater inspired by Thalia, the Greek Muse of comedy; to Shakespeare's *Much Ado About Nothing,* to the modern *Shakespeare in Love.*

So together or alone, with friends or with family, to enhance a new love or revive an old one, or maybe even realize you really want to be alone for a while... use this book to select the best romantic comedy for your situation.

This rom-com movie guide can help you find the perfect film to match your mood, to put you in a different mood, bring up things you find hard to talk about, start conversations that can clear up misunderstandings, and just generally improve your romantic well-being.

You too can use romantic comedies to make a difference in your love life.

SECTION ONE

"Love is never lost. If not reciprocated, it will flow back and soften and purify the heart."

WASHINGTON IRVING, *author of "The Legend of Sleepy Hollow" and "Rip Van Winkle"*

CHAPTER 1

Am I Good Enough to Be Loved?

ANNIE HALL

RELEASE DATE

1977

BRIEF DESCRIPTION

Insecure guy Woody Allen falls for scatterbrained Diane Keaton but lets his own, and her, neuroses get in the way of what might have been a good match.

CAST

Woody Allen (Alvy Singer), Diane Keaton (Annie Hall)

LOVER TYPES

Insecure / Self-Sabotaging / Shallow / Ditzy / Fearful of Failure / Fearful of Success

- You might actually be more attractive than you feel you are.
- Give it more than one try.
- Focus on the feelings between you, not just your own feelings.

QUOTABLE

Woody Allen: I would never want to belong to any club that would have someone like me for a member. That's the key joke of my adult life, in terms of my relationships with women.

THE STORY

Woody Allen embodies insecurity on every level from work to looks to romance. Our relationships are mirrors in which we see ourselves reflected. That's both the good news and the bad news. He has so many doubts about himself and his self-worth that he sabotages his relationship with ditzy Diane Keaton. It's all funny... in a rather sad kind of way. For the more secure person it can get quite emotionally draining having to always reassure the insecure person. Unfortunately, it can also begin to plant serious doubts in that more secure person. Finding a way to appreciate one's own worth and not count on others to do it may help save a relationship.

MY BIG FAT GREEK WEDDING

NIA VARDALOS:

Why?... Why do you love me?

JOHN CORBETT:

Because I came alive when I met you.

RELEASE DATE

2002

BRIEF DESCRIPTION

Nia Vardalos is insecure but chafes at her family's expectations and dares to accept a date outside her culture. Then she dares to believe John Corbett actually might really love her.

CAST

Nia Vardalos (Toula Portokalos), John Corbett (Ian Miller)

LOVER TYPES

Used to Being the Unattractive One / Family and Tradition-Bound / Shy / Free of Conventions on Beauty / Willing to Walk into Unfamiliar Situations for the Sake of Love

- Cultures clash, but real love is deeply heart-to-heart.
- Be persistent in breaking down others' preconceived notions.
- Learn to love yourself. Sometimes because others do; sometimes so others can.

QUOTABLE

Nia Vardalos: Why?... Why do you love me?
John Corbett: Because I came alive when I met you.

THE STORY

Nia Vardalos is a young Greek woman used to being the "not pretty" girl. She's certainly not used to men finding her attractive and at thirty she's got lots of pressure from her large family to get married to a nice Greek boy. Instead she falls for decidedly non-Greek John Corbett and to her growing delight he rather seems to like her. A lot. Unbelievable! John has to face the challenge of being good enough for her protective father and the extended tradition-bound family. Nia is challenged to accept that someone she likes actually likes her back... and that it is turning to love. Her transformation from being insecure to being rapturously in love is inspiring for anyone unsure of their own worth. Part of that freedom is realizing that with so many people who love her, she is also worthy of her own self-love.

AMÉLIE

RELEASE DATE
2001

BRIEF DESCRIPTION
Audrey Tautou longs for love but is too shy to reach out for it or expect it. Once she starts helping others find love, though, there's plenty to go around for her, too.

CAST
Audrey Tautou (Amélie Poulain), Serge Merlin (Raymond Dufayel), Mathieu Kassovitz (Nino Quincampoix)

LOVER TYPES
Introvert / Longing for Love / Disillusioned / Naïve / Obsessive / Romantic / Insecure

SERGE MERLIN:
You mean she would rather imagine herself relating to an absent person than build relationships with those around her?

- Real love comes first from inside ourselves.
- Making love can happen in many ways —
  including helping others find love.
- When you connect with the Love that
  permeates all creation you realize you are
  an important part of that.

Serge Merlin: You mean she would rather
imagine herself relating to an absent
person than build relationships with those
around her?

Audrey Tautou is a very shy young woman
who yearns for love and affection but, having
grown up with a cold and distant father and
having lost her mother at a young age, she
has always felt alone and does not think
she is worthy of love. Her self-doubt keeps
her from facing the realities of the world.
Her older neighbor Serge Merlin paints the
same copy of a famous painting over and
over, never quite getting one of the girls in
it right. Sharing an insecurity about their
worth and their talent, he is nonetheless able
to ask her questions that begin to shake her
out of her fear of not being good enough
to experience real life. And she offers him
insights into what the young woman in the
painting may be feeling, such that he is finally
able to artistically capture her. Sometimes we
can gain in self-worth by helping others feel
worthy — and that's always a worthy cause.

HITCH

KEVIN JAMES:

You know what it's like getting up every morning feeling hopeless...?

RELEASE DATE

2005

BRIEF DESCRIPTION

Dating coach Will Smith helps painfully shy Kevin James gain the confidence to pursue the woman of his dreams. It actually works, and Will himself learns more about love along the way.

CAST

Will Smith (Hitch), Kevin James (Albert), Eva Mendes (Sara)

LOVER TYPES

Cocky / Unrequited / Hopeless / Oblivious to Others' Affections / Surface-Focused / Wanting the Very Best for the Other / Willing to Learn

- Real love is wanting the very best for the beloved, even if it hurts you.
- Why not dream big? That plus doing the work may well get you positive results.
- Learn to play the outer games of love and you can gain the confidence to reach for the deeper rewards of really loving.

QUOTABLE

Kevin James: You know what it's like getting up every morning feeling hopeless, feeling like the love of your life is waking up with the wrong man? But at the same time, hoping that she still finds happiness, even if it's never going to be with you?

THE STORY

Will Smith coaches men on romance. Instilling self-confidence is a must. His client Kevin James is an insecure, rather ordinary guy with a serious crush on a gorgeous woman waaaay out of his league. Maybe. This fun story centers on the two men and how they build up Kevin's self-worth such that he catches the attention of the lady of his dreams and guess what — they actually do get together, quite happily. The message we learn from the guys in this film is that dreaming big actually can work if you have integrity... and get out of your own way.

CHAPTER 2

The Broken Hearts Club — How to Cancel Your Membership

MUST LOVE DOGS

JOHN CUSACK:

I think your heart grows back bigger...

RELEASE DATE

2005

BRIEF DESCRIPTION

Hopeless romantic John Cusack would rather feel pain than feel nothing at all. When he and divorcée Diane Lane meet and start to fall for each other, both must be willing to start healing their broken hearts and go for joy for a change.

CAST

John Cusack (Jake), Diane Lane (Sarah Nolan)

LOVER TYPES

Hopeless Romantic / Martyr to Love's Pain / Divorced and Mourning It / Hopeful Re-Dater

LOVE LESSONS

- Feeling something, even pain, is better than feeling nothing.
- Believing in romantic love can bring you elevated joy, even when it kind of hurts, too.
- Pain and heartbreak can heighten the intensity of love... up to a point.

QUOTABLE

John Cusack: I think your heart grows back bigger... all this pain and heartache that you go through and you gotta go through... to come out to a better place and that's how I see it, anyway.

THE STORY

John Cusack is a hopeless romantic with a broken heart. He rather seems to relish the pain and also seems determined to get something positive from it. When he meets divorcée Diane Lane, who's hesitantly stepping back into dating, we wonder how these two people with broken hearts and disappointed dreams might work out together. John's desire to keep feeling, even if it's painful, leads him toward feeling love and joy again. He's also not afraid to talk about his feelings to his friends. He believes you can make something wonderful out of the pain of a broken heart — and then proves it. So can we.

THE BREAK-UP

JON FAVREAU :

That poor girl never stood a chance.

RELEASE DATE

2006

BRIEF DESCRIPTION

Jennifer Aniston breaks up with immature Vince Vaughan to make him be more attentive, but he thinks she really doesn't love him anymore and that breaks his heart as they drift further apart.

CAST

Jennifer Aniston (Brooke Meyers), Vince Vaughan (Gary Grobowski), Jon Favreau (Johnny O)

LOVER TYPES

Eternally Immature / Dissatisfied / Needy / Clueless / Inside a Protective Shell / Having Unrealistic Expectations

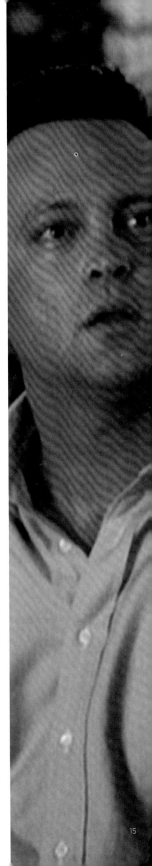

- No one can read minds, so tell them what you feel, think, and need.
- Trying to manipulate others usually leads to disappointment and worse.
- Keeping your heart closed won't keep it safe from being broken.

QUOTABLE

Jon Favreau to Vince Vaughan: Everybody thinks that they're your friend, but the fact of the matter is that there's not one person I know that you trust enough to let close enough that they could hurt you. And her big problem is that you really liked her. I mean she is the one girl you really liked. And no matter what she did and how she tried, you were never gonna let your guard down. That poor girl never stood a chance.

THE STORY

Jennifer Aniston has broken up with her boyfriend, Vince Vaughan, in hopes he'll learn to really appreciate her. He thinks she's really breaking up and as they vie over who'll get their co-owned condo the misunderstandings and disappointments grow. Each of them thinks the other doesn't care enough to change and keep them together. If only both of them had the courage to say how they really feel and listen to what the other has to say... but their broken hearts rule the day. Until maybe a few months later when they meet again and there might just be some little sparks still flying. What do we learn here? Don't expect your partner to read your mind; tell them what you really feel and think, and be willing to listen to what they really feel and think. Don't let a lack of real communication sabotage what may be a very real love.

(500) DAYS OF SUMMER

JOSEPH GORDON-LEVITT :
*... you just replay it
in your head over
and over again ...*

2009

BRIEF DESCRIPTION

Joseph Gordon-Levitt is
caught in the hamster wheel
of overanalyzing his failed
relationship with Zooey
Deschanel but finally finds the
hope to try for love again.

CAST

Joseph Gordon-Levitt (Tom),
Zooey Deschanel (Summer)

LOVER TYPES

Obsessive Romantic /
Disinterested in Love / Love
Denier / Naïve / Analysis
Paralysis

LOVE LESSONS

- There may not be any specific discoverable cause of why love didn't work, so just accept it and move on.
- Don't let past failures keep you from trying again.
- Learn what you can from your own and others' mistakes and be alert to the signs that it probably isn't going to work.

QUOTABLE

Joseph Gordon-Levitt: Do you ever do this, you think back on all the times you've had with someone and you just replay it in your head over and over again and you look for those first signs of trouble?

THE STORY

When your heart is broken, it's easy to get fixated on examining and reexamining every little incident, phrase, and look that might have led to what brought about the breakup. Naïvely romantic Joseph Gordon-Levitt spends an awful lot of time in forensic-romance-land in this movie, trying to figure out what went wrong in his failed relationship with love-cynic Zooey Deschanel. Maybe some of our loves are just doomed from the beginning but unless we see that, we're on our way to getting our heart ripped out. Joseph shows us that even a broken, bleeding heart can be hopeful and might just love again, in another season and, hopefully, with a better reason this time.

UNDER THE TUSCAN SUN

DIANE LANE:
Do you know the most surprising thing about divorce? It doesn't actually kill you.

RELEASE DATE
2003

BRIEF DESCRIPTION
Diane Lane is reeling from an unexpected divorce and goes to Italy to recover. She begins to heal her broken heart by diving into a fix-it project, warming to the locals, and helping others find love.

CAST
Diane Lane (Frances), Raoul Bova (Marcello), Sandra Oh (Patti)

LOVER TYPES
Divorced and Still in Shock / The Tall Dark Stranger / Young Lovers from Different Cultures / Platonic

- A broken heart is really difficult to heal; give yourself credit for even being willing to try again.
- Change and creative projects can re-stimulate your own romantic energies. Fix a thing and you begin to fix yourself.
- Helping others find love can open your eyes to new love for you.

QUOTABLE

Diane Lane: Do you know the most surprising thing about divorce? It doesn't actually kill you. Like a bullet to the heart or a head-on car wreck. It should. When someone you've promised to cherish till death do you part says, "I never loved you," it should kill you instantly. ... I must have known, of course, but I was too scared to see the truth.

THE STORY

Diane Lane is in shock from an unexpected divorce and takes up her friends' offer of a trip to Italy to try to pull herself together. She then takes on the restoration of a house in Tuscany and in tandem with making that physical structure livable, begins a healing process for herself. Her kindness and generosity with local workers and neighbors yields new friends and she begins to open her heart again. A lesson for the brokenhearted — don't wallow too long in your own mess because it can set the wrong pattern. Try a change of scenery, be open to accepting care and kindness from others, take on a new creative project, reach out to others in friendly non-romantic ways, and before too long you might find your own heart, like her house under the Tuscan sun, a place once again fit for romance to inhabit.

CHAPTER 3

Want More Love?
Give More Love!

NOTTING HILL

HUGH GRANT:
... she was just a girl, standing in front of a boy, asking him to love her.

RELEASE DATE
1999

BRIEF DESCRIPTION
The life of simple bookshop owner Hugh Grant changes when he meets Julia Roberts, the most famous film star in the world. Used to always getting lots of love, when she learns to actually give love her life changes too.

CAST
Hugh Grant (William Thacker), Julia Roberts (Anna Scott)

LOVER TYPES
Strong Independent Successful Professional / Distrustful of Others' Motives / Shy / Insecure / Dares to Dream / Kind and Forgiving

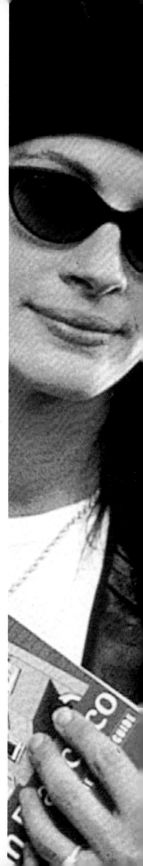

- You have to be willing to give what you want to get.
- You may not be a big movie star, but you certainly want and deserve love.
- True love requires being vulnerable and accepting the other person's vulnerability too.

QUOTABLE

Hugh Grant: It was sort of sweet actually. I mean, I know she's an actress and all that, so she can deliver a line. But she said that she might be as famous as can be — but also... that she was just a girl, standing in front of a boy, asking him to love her.

THE STORY

Movie actress Julia Roberts finds it hard to trust anyone in matters of the heart, and no wonder, given her spotty romantic history and the constant scrutiny of the paparazzi. Even her tender close encounter with shy local man Hugh Grant is ruined when the press discovers it. Julia leaves. But her own desires for true love bring her back and she reaches out to give love, regardless of what she may get in return. And for an image-conscious international superstar, nothing says "unconditional love" more than sitting beside your boutique bookstore-owning boyfriend in a movie theater — when he's wearing swimming goggles because he can't find his regular glasses.

GROUND-HOG DAY

BILL MURRAY:
I couldn't imagine a better fate than a long and lustrous winter.

RELEASE DATE
1993

BRIEF DESCRIPTION
Narcissist Bill Murray is trapped in a repeat of the same day until he learns to see other people as real, valuable individuals worthy of recognition, respect, and love.

CAST
Bill Murray (Phil), Andie MacDowell (Rita)

LOVER TYPES
Arrogant / Narcissistic / Selfish / Patient / Hopeful / Resigned / Forgiving

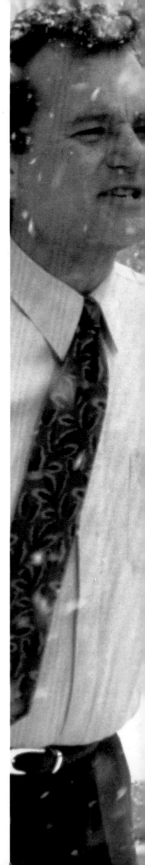

LOVE LESSONS

- It's really not all about you. Even if you think it is.
- Other people's lives and love can enrich your own life... so very much.
- Have the patience to explore what really means the most in any life.

QUOTABLE

Bill Murray: When Chekhov saw the long winter, he saw a winter bleak and dark and bereft of hope. Yet we know that winter is just another step in the cycle of life. But standing here among the people of Punxsutawney and basking in the warmth of their hearths and hearts, I couldn't imagine a better fate than a long and lustrous winter.

THE STORY

Self-centered TV weather celebrity Bill Murray is "all about me" all the time. But trapped in a repeating loop of living the same day over and over and over, he finally begins to realize that other people might have some actual worth other than as accessories and an audience to his own life. As he begins to open up to others and actually starts reaching out to help and encourage people in their own goals and save them from the accidents and missteps he's seen them make again and again, his heart begins to warm. Bill experiences the first glimmers of the joy of really connecting to other people in authentic, caring ways. His is a funny and poignant journey from selfish no love to giving love to getting love, including a romantic relationship with Andie MacDowell. Just hope you don't have to make your own transformation all on the same day over and over again.

AMÉLIE

NARRATOR:
Amélie has a strange feeling of absolute harmony.

RELEASE DATE
2001

BRIEF DESCRIPTION
Introvert Amélie dares to venture out into the world and help others find the love she herself has not found. Unsurprisingly, her generosity brings more love into her own life.

CAST
Audrey Tautou (Amélie Poulain), Serge Merlin (Raymond Doufayel), Mathieu Kassovitz (Nino Quincampoix)

LOVER TYPES
Introvert / Longing for Love / Disillusioned / Naïve / Obsessive / Romantic / Insecure

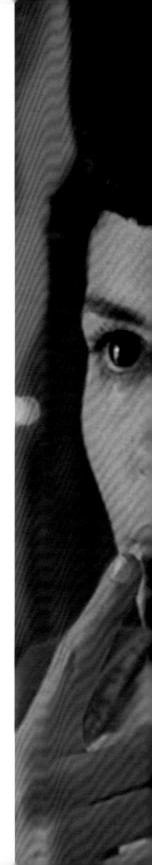

- Nature and the cosmos are abundant and when you tap into that you have an endless source of love.
- Being willing to sacrifice your own well-being for that of others is an act that often brings great rewards.
- It's always a good idea to chase down the possibility of ideal love, just in case it actually happens.

QUOTABLE

Narrator: Amélie has a strange feeling of absolute harmony. It's a perfect moment. A soft light, a scent in the air, the quiet murmur of the city. A surge of love, an urge to help mankind overcomes her.

THE STORY

Amélie is a painfully shy young woman who decides to help other people find happiness since she can only imagine herself in a romantic relationship but doesn't believe it could ever happen to her in real life. Using her keen sense of observation of others, she performs targeted acts of kindness that propel those individuals into new ways of thinking and feeling. In the process her own heart begins to open with generous love, and her soon-to-be-lover sees the glow in her and begins a pursuit to discover her identity. By living out her ideal of love, Amélie brings joy to others of all ages and inclinations, and along the way, her own dream of personal romantic love comes true. What a great example of how when we give to others we get so much more in return.

JERRY MAGUIRE

RENÉE ZELLWEGER:
I love him for the man he wants to be.

RELEASE DATE
1996

BRIEF DESCRIPTION
Shy Renée Zellweger idolizes cocky sports agent Tom Cruise. When he goes all idealistic and is unceremoniously tossed from his company, she follows and offers to help build his new freelance agency. He is in dire need of unconditional love and she just might be able to provide it.

CAST
Tom Cruise (Jerry Maguire), Renée Zellweger (Dorothy Boyd), Cuba Gooding Jr. (Rod Tidwell)

LOVER TYPES
Type A Ambitious / Shy Admirer / The Realistic One / Insecure / "Not My Type"

- You may not be quite right in who you think the other person is.
- Giving love without specific expectation is both scary and powerful.
- Holding fast to your ideal of the other person might actually help them to live up to that ideal.

Renée Zellweger: I love him! I love him for the man he wants to be. And I love him for the man he almost is.

Both Tom Cruise and Renée Zellweger are in need of more love. Tom, possessed by a fit of idealism, stepped away from a powerful job and is trying to make it as an independent sports agent. Renée, possessed by hero worship and a strong personal attraction, follows and dedicates herself to his new business. Tom has an instant rapport with Renée's young son and she begins to see more of his passion for his work; his so-far only client, Cuba Gooding Jr.; and his desire to be a better man. Though both are vulnerable and scared to open up to love, they each take the chance and give love to the other. She offers him a sense of worth and dignity. He offers her acceptance and a real joy for living. It works and everybody wins!

CHAPTER 4

Starting Over?
You Want to Get Back
in the Game, But...

MUST LOVE DOGS

JOHN CUSACK:

A love so real even after you're dead it still hurts. That's what I want.

RELEASE DATE
2005

BRIEF DESCRIPTION

John Cusack is a guy so wounded he loves his wound. Can he possibly get over that and actually move into the world of real romance again?

CAST

John Cusack (Jake), Diane Lane (Sarah Nolan)

LOVER TYPES

Hopeless Romantic / Martyr to Love's Pain / Divorced and Mourning It / Hopeful Re-Dater /

- The intensity of real love lost may well be worth the pain... but don't stay there too long lest you miss the rewards of real-life love.
- Be brave enough to dare to love again.
- Some people thrive on desire, some on fulfillment. Figure out which one you are.

QUOTABLE

John Cusack: It's all there, man. The yearning, the suffering, a woman you pursue through blizzards across continents. A love so real even after you're dead it still hurts. That's what I want.

THE STORY

Yearning. Unrequited love. The desire to desire. The drive to become worthy of an unobtainable love. Suffering for love. These are feelings that throughout history have often been transformed into great (and sometimes not so great) art. John Cusack dares to take his broken heart out into the world of possibilities again, even if one of those possibilities is that he'll get his heart broken again. Once he finds the courage to start over and yearn again, he finds someone worth yearning over. Before too long, lo and behold, they actually get together and yearning leads to fulfillment. Be brave enough to yearn in spite of what has happened before and you, too, may well find that "love so real."

SLEEP-LESS IN SEATTLE

TOM HANKS:

*I just want somebody
I can have a decent
conversation with
over dinner.*

RELEASE DATE

1993

BRIEF DESCRIPTION

Tom Hanks clings to the memory of his late wife and their magical marriage while across the country Meg Ryan is dissatisfied with her non-magical fiancé. With an entire continent and a lot of emotional hesitation and expectation between them what could possibly bring them together? A young boy, a radio talk show, and the dream of true love.

CAST

Tom Hanks (Sam Baldwin), Meg Ryan (Annie Reed)

LOVER TYPES

Grieving / Lonely / Clinging to a Memory of Lost Love / Confused / Unsure About What or Who They Really Want / Hesitant / Afraid to Love and Lose Again

LOVE LESSONS

- Though you can never replace the person who died there may well be a new person with a new kind of love that is also magical in its own special way.
- Don't settle for less than the magic.
- Don't let miles, other people, or your own fears keep you from taking those first steps toward starting over.

QUOTABLE

Tom Hanks: Well, I'm not looking for a mail-order bride! I just want somebody I can have a decent conversation with over dinner. Without it falling down into weepy tears over some movie!

THE STORY

Tom Hanks's young son wants his lonely, widowed father to start dating and find a woman to marry so they can be a whole family again. The boy calls in to a romance advice radio show and gets his dad to start talking about how much he loved his wife, how his heart is broken, and how he's not ready to start over yet. Across the country Meg Ryan hears the show and becomes more and more interested in this man on the verge of starting over. So much so that she breaks up with her straitlaced fiancé. After false starts and much hesitancy they finally agree to meet atop the Empire State Building. And it works! Sometimes our love for those we love, like Tom's for his son, is the catalyst to get us out again in the search for new romantic love. Starting over sometimes means just deciding it's okay to do so. Sometimes it means a physical journey. Always it requires courage to try again for the magic. And sometimes as a bonus you get a great view from high above a magnificent city.

UNDER THE TUSCAN SUN

DIANE LANE:

Unthinkably good things can happen even late in the game.

RELEASE DATE

2003

BRIEF DESCRIPTION

Devastated by a sudden divorce, Diane Lane is not looking for love when she moves to Italy but, surrounded by others' love, she begins to think about starting over again.

CAST

Diane Lane (Frances), Raoul Bova (Marcello), Sandra Oh (Patti)

LOVER TYPES

Divorced and Still in Shock / The Tall Dark Stranger / Young Lovers from Different Cultures / Platonic / A Person from Your Past

- Just because that one someone dumped you doesn't mean you're totally unlovable.
- Remember the "start" in starting over and don't expect to immediately have a full-blown relationship. The journey starts from where you are, one step at a time.
- Pay attention when others pay attention to you; they may well be seeing something you've forgotten you have.

QUOTABLE

Diane Lane: Unthinkably good things can happen even late in the game. It's such a surprise.

THE STORY

Recently divorced Diane Lane comes to Italy to recover from a broken heart but with no intention of starting over with romance. Once she buys and starts restoring an old house in Tuscany she begins opening up to life and joy again through her interactions with local craftsmen and friendly neighbors. She even takes on a crusade to persuade a village girl's father that his daughter's romance with a Polish worker might well be a good thing. Without even meaning to, she steps onto the path of starting over. Breaking that ring-pass-not of passionate encounters with an attractive Italian man, Diane then seems free to look up and out again for possible new love. She just may have found it in a fellow American writer she knew long ago. The lesson for us: Sometimes starting over just sneaks up on you. Be open to that and who knows what other wonderful things may happen along the way.

THE APART-MENT

SHIRLEY MACLAINE:
Shut up and deal.

RELEASE DATE
1960

BRIEF DESCRIPTION
Jack Lemmon loans out his apartment for illicit affairs but finds himself falling in love with the mistress of one of his bosses.

CAST
Shirley MacLaine (Fran Kubelik), Jack Lemmon (C. C. Baxter), Fred MacMurray (Jeff D. Sheldrake)

LOVER TYPES
Naïve / Disillusioned / Insecure / Compromising / Hopeful / Nice Guy

- Be savvy about the signs of someone's dishonesty and cheating.
- Don't let a bad mistake in judgment about love ruin the rest of your life.
- What looks like "just a faithful friend" could be your next love.

QUOTABLE

Shirley MacLaine: Shut up and deal.

THE STORY

Jack Lemmon is a mid-level manager who reluctantly loans out his city apartment to married higher-ups to use for their adulterous affairs, hoping to get a promotion out of it. He grows fond of elevator girl Shirley MacLaine and they strike up a sweet friendship, often playing spirited card games together. He doesn't know she's the current mistress of Fred MacMurray, one of his bosses who is also using the apartment for their affair. Shirley doesn't know she's only the latest in a long string of mistresses and when she finds out, she breaks it off with Fred, even though she's in love with him. After the deceit, disillusionment, and disappointment of her affair with a married man, and after Jack saves her from an overdose, Shirley looks at her friend with new eyes. By the act of initiating a card game Shirley signals she is ready to overcome her own past and start over, and Jack is very happy about that. Very happy indeed. It often happens that the means to start over has been right there in front of us all the time. All we need to do is deal a new hand.

CHAPTER 5

Again... ? Should You Really Reconnect with Your Ex?

THE PHILA-DELPHIA STORY

KATHARINE HEPBURN:

I don't want to be worshiped, I want to be loved.

RELEASE DATE

1940

BRIEF DESCRIPTION

Socialite Katharine Hepburn has three men on her hands just before her wedding and is faced with making the right choice between her ex-husband, her next husband, and an admiring reporter.

CAST

Katharine Hepburn (Tracy Lord), Cary Grant (C. K. Dexter Haven), Jimmy Stewart (Macaulay Connor)

LOVER TYPES

Spoiled / Flighty / Judgmental / Cocky / Worshipful / Persistent

- Figure out who you really are and what you really want.
- Don't let other people's expectations keep you from that.
- If the mutual passion is still there — go for it.

QUOTABLE

Katharine Hepburn: I don't want to be worshipped, I want to be loved.

THE STORY

Society girl Katharine Hepburn and her former hubby, Cary Grant, are thrown back together on the eve of her wedding to a wealthy but boring man. Jimmy Stewart is a reporter who also falls for Katharine and helps her learn more about who she really is. Dialogue back then was quite smart and full of innuendo while still being very accessible, which makes every conversation ever so much fun while seeming to be very proper. It's a rom-com recipe for up-and-down emotions, snappy dialogue, misunderstandings, and a reevaluation of what is most important in marriage. Turns out it's mutual passionate love! Who'd have thought? If the fire is still there, it may well still be worth exploring.

MAMMA MIA!

PIERCE BROSNAN:

There's no hurry anymore, when all is said and done...

RELEASE DATE

2008

BRIEF DESCRIPTION

Pierce Brosnan returns to the island where he last saw Meryl Streep, invited by the girl who may be their daughter. She's still hurt he left her twenty years ago; he still thinks she left him.

CAST

Meryl Streep (Donna), Pierce Brosnan (Sam)

LOVER TYPES

No Time or Trust for Love / Holding on to the Hurt / Yearning to Reconnect / Afraid to Be Left Again

LOVE LESSONS

- If you don't know the whole story, you can't really make a good decision.
- A true love can stand the test of time, even if all that time was spent apart.
- What you idolized years ago still shines, despite the time gone by.

QUOTABLE

Pierce Brosnan: Deep inside, both of us could feel the autumn chill... when the summer's over and the dark clouds hide the sun, neither you nor I'm to blame when all is said and done. In our lives, we have walked some strange and lonely treks, slightly worn but dignified and not too old for sex. Standing calmly at the crossroads, no desire to run. There's no hurry anymore, when all is said and done.*

THE STORY

Meryl Streep and Pierce Brosnan were lovers twenty years ago, then lost track of each other. Now brought back together by their (possible) daughter's desire to know her father, they dance around the growing realization that they are still each other's one true love. Though their daughter decides not to marry but to travel with her lover and have great adventures, the older couple step up to the altar, say their vows, and go for it. After all, love is love and even with dignity, passion is still passion and not to be turned away.

* Written by Björn Ulvaeus specifically for the movie soundtrack and added to the song's original lyrics as recorded by ABBA first in 1981.

HIS GIRL FRIDAY

CARY GRANT:

There's been a lamp burning in the window for ya, honey....

RELEASE DATE

1940

BRIEF DESCRIPTION

News reporter Rosalind Russell thinks she wants a quiet domestic life but just before her marriage, ex-husband Cary Grant lures her back into action on a big breaking story.

CAST

Cary Grant (Walter Burns), Rosalind Russell (Hildy Johnson)

LOVER TYPES

Savvy / Cocky / Type A / Business Pro / Wanting to Change / Seeking Stability

LOVE LESSONS

- Excitement and a life of purpose is addictive and not easily left behind.
- Don't waste your talents or your time trying to become what you're not.
- Stay connected with who and what makes you feel most alive.

QUOTABLE

Cary Grant: There's been a lamp burning in the window for ya, honey....
Rosalind Russell: Oh, I jumped out that window a long time ago.
Cary: We've got something between us nothing can change.

THE STORY

Big-city newspaper reporters Rosalind Russell and Cary Grant had been married; then she divorced him. Now she's about to marry a mild-mannered insurance man but Cary wants to draw her back in to help with a big news scoop. And maybe win her back. She's torn between going for a normal domestic life or the high-energy excitement of reporting on things that really matter. She's also torn between a calm marriage and getting back together with a man who stirs her soul and fires her ambitions. Thanks to the news story and all it stirs up, Rosalind can now choose wisely — she steps back into passion.

IT'S COMPLICATED

ALEC BALDWIN:
I don't regret giving it another shot.

RELEASE DATE
2009

BRIEF DESCRIPTION
Thrown together ten years after their divorce, Meryl Streep and Alec Baldwin fall into a fling, though he's remarried and she's with someone too.

CAST
Meryl Streep (Jane Adler), Alec Baldwin (Jake Adler)

LOVER TYPES
Playboy / Nostalgic / Fun-Loving / Questing and Questioning / Open to Exploration

- It takes more than just attraction to make a marriage work.
- You can honor the good parts of your past without having to return to it.
- If what split you apart is still part of the equation, it's probably not going to change.

Alec Baldwin: I don't regret giving it another shot.

Meryl Streep: It probably would have worked, if you hadn't been married.

Alec Baldwin: I wouldn't have considered it, if I wasn't!

Meryl Streep: I don't regret it either.

Meryl Streep and Alec Baldwin were married. Now they're divorced and he's remarried, while she's the object of Steve Martin's romantic attentions. When they're thrown together at their son's graduation, the sparks fly again and they have a fling. A rather passionate fling. A fling woven through with joy. An ongoing fling that just might bring them back together. But though the attraction is still strong, they know each other just a little too well and both realize it's better all around for everyone concerned if they do not continue the affair. Sometimes the ideal solution is to just let it go.

SECTION TWO

"Love is space and time measured by the heart."

MARCEL PROUST, *author of* Remembrance of Things Past

CHAPTER 6

Young Love

LOVE ACTUALLY

LIAM NEESON:

Aren't you a bit young to be in love?

RELEASE DATE

2003

BRIEF DESCRIPTION

Young Sam has lost his mom but has fallen in love with classmate Olivia. What's he willing to risk to declare his love?

CAST

Liam Neeson (Daniel), Thomas Sangster (Sam), Olivia Olson (Joanna Anderson)

LOVER TYPES

Very Young Love / Grieving / Innocent / Hopeful / Oblivious

LOVE LESSONS

- Go for it. Really. Just go for it. Seriously, what do you have to lose?

- Your first love really counts because it sets the pattern for all the other loves of your life. Choose carefully, but with high ideals and joy.
- Realize and appreciate that young love inspires you to explore new areas.

Thomas Sangster: Okay. Well, the truth is... actually... I'm in love.
Liam Neeson: Sorry?
Thomas Sangster: I know I should be thinking about Mum all the time, and I am. But the truth is, I'm in love and I was before she died, and there's nothing I can do about it.
Liam Neeson: Aren't you a bit young to be in love?
Thomas Sangster: No.
Liam Neeson: Oh, well, okay... right. Well, I mean, I'm a little relieved.
Thomas Sangster: Why?
Liam Neeson: Well, because I thought it would be something worse.
Thomas Sangster: Worse than the total agony of being in love?
Liam Neeson: Oh. No, you're right. Yeah, total agony.

THE STORY

Young Thomas Sangster's mother has died and his stepdad, Liam Neeson, is raising him alone. Thomas has a huge crush on classmate Olivia Olson, a talented singer who he thinks doesn't even know he's alive. In a bid to get her attention he takes up the drums, much to Liam's dismay about the noise. But he supports the boy's yearnings. While he's playing onstage in her band at a Christmas concert, Thomas thinks Olivia singles him out for attention but it's just her performance. Liam urges him to go after Olivia and tell her how he feels before she leaves the country. They rush to the airport and Thomas sprints through security to catch her. It's a very sweet moment as they smile at each other and she gives him a kiss. Thomas beams with pride and joy. One of the best things about chivalric love is that it can drive us to be better than we were in order to be worthy of the love object. For Thomas it is learning a new skill and being brave enough to go after what he wants. What would it be for you?

GREASE

RELEASE DATE

1978

BRIEF DESCRIPTION

Innocent Olivia Newton-John and bad boy John Travolta enjoy a summer romance that fractures against the realities of different high school cliques. Can they reach across that gulf and really be together again?

CAST

Olivia Newton-John (Sandy), John Travolta (Danny)

LOVER TYPES

Innocent / Sweet / Rebel / Cocky Outside, Sentimental Inside

LOVE LESSONS

- What's more important than being cool? Being real!

OLIVIA NEWTON-JOHN:

My heart is saying, "Don't let go."

- And often on the flip side, daring to explore different aspects of yourself can make you cool.
- You don't want to be a slave to your peers but, often, learning to adapt to play the games of different cultures can bring fun rewards.

QUOTABLE

Olivia Newton-John: My head is saying, "Fool, forget him." My heart is saying, "Don't let go. Hold on till the end." And that's what I intend to do. I'm hopelessly devoted to you. But now there's nowhere to hide, since you pushed my love aside. I'm out of my head, hopelessly devoted to you.*

THE STORY

Yearning, yielding, losing, weeping, hoping, all in high dramatic emotion... that's young love. Olivia Newton-John is an innocent high schooler from Australia who had a summer love with local bad boy John Travolta. Now back in classes he brags about the romance but is startled when Olivia shows up at his school, rather than having moved back home. Even though he's crazy about her, he denies their love, knowing he'd lose his "cool" to have fallen for a sweet girl like her. Olivia moons around and gets loosen-up advice from some of the wilder girls. This young love is doomed unless one of them changes. In a fun nostalgic musical romp through an idealized California high school Olivia finally trades in "innocent" for "cool," and really enjoys it — especially since it brings her and John back together. A teenager's job is to break away from their family to explore and embrace new identities. It's fortunate when the spur to do that is love — which is, after all, meant to radically change us. Even if the romance doesn't work out, the young, malleable heart is changed for having been in love.

* Written by John Farrar for the film; nominated for an Academy Award for Best Original Song.

MY FATHER THE HERO

KATHERINE HEIGL:
I told him you were my lover.

GÉRARD DEPARDIEU:
Are you serious?

RELEASE DATE
1994

BRIEF DESCRIPTION
Indulgent father Gérard Depardieu goes along with teen daughter Katherine Heigl's fiction that he's her lover, all to impress a boy. Then things get even more complicated.

CAST
Gérard Depardieu (Andre), Katherine Heigl (Nicole), Dalton James (Ben)

LOVER TYPES
Yearning Teen / Indulgent Parent / Confused / Desperate / Truly Caring

LOVE LESSONS
- When desperate we'll often take desperate measures; not always a wise idea.

- Lies, even for a seemingly good cause, are seldom a very good plan.
- Willingness to sacrifice for each other, even in romance, can strengthen family ties.

Katherine Heigl: I told Ben you weren't my father.
Gérard Depardieu: Why?
Katherine Heigl: Because I wanted to impress him.
Gérard Depardieu: What did you tell him I was? A famous pianist? A writer? What?
Katherine Heigl: I told him you were my lover.
Gérard Depardieu: Are you serious?

THE STORY

Fourteen-year-old Katherine Heigl is on vacation in the Bahamas with her divorced father, Gérard Depardieu, who's trying to bond with her after years of separation. She is trying to make herself more attractive and sophisticated to the boy she's set her sights on so she tells people that her father is her lover. Eyebrows raise and whiffs of scandal swirl. Trying to be a supportive father, Gérard eventually goes along and coaches his daughter on how to win a guy, meanwhile moving forward in his desire to be closer to his own girlfriend back in Paris. The boy she likes is puzzled that Katherine would be with a much older man but all is revealed when he's in danger and she calls him "Dad." When young we'll try just about anything to win love. With our children, we'll often do just about anything to ensure their happiness. In this rom-com all sorts out well as young love triumphs and parental love strengthens. Respecting the desires of young people in love and helping them realize those in healthy ways can help build better relationships all around.

BIG

RELEASE DATE
1988

BRIEF DESCRIPTION
Thirteen-year-old Tom Hanks is magically made thirty, gets a dream job at a toy company plus a dream girlfriend. He's great at handling the former, and at a loss handling the latter. What's a boy to do?

CAST
Tom Hanks (Josh), Elizabeth Perkins (Susan)

LOVER TYPES
Pubescent / Naïve / Confused / Entranced

LOVE LESSONS
- Love, like growing up, progresses in its own time. Don't try to rush it or you might miss some of the most important steps.

- A sense of childish wonder is a love bonus for anyone at any age.
- Try to look at others (and yourself) with a very wide scope of who they were, who they are, and who they may become. Then try to realize which one of those is in action at any given time and your relationships may well be enriched.

QUOTABLE

Tom Hanks's Boss: You can't keep a kid from growing up. All a thirteen-year-old boy wants is a thirteen-year-old girl. And I sure don't know how to build one of those.

THE STORY

Tom Hanks is a thirteen-year-old boy who wishes on a magic machine to be bigger. Imagine his surprise when he wakes up in an adult body. He gets a job at a toy company where coworker Elizabeth Perkins falls for thirtyish Tom. He falls for her, too, but in his naïveté treats her like a girl his real age. Love is confusing in this pretzel twist of young love; older love being offered to a young heart in an adult body; and Tom's eventual desire to return to his younger, innocent self so he doesn't miss anything in between — such as young love between two people who are both actually young. Younger people in love often feel older and more grown up, while older people often find that being in love makes them feel young again. This film gives us both sides of that dynamic and offers some excellent advice for anyone of any age: Hang on to your joy for life, your zest for adventure, and your appreciation of other people. It'll serve you well, no matter how old you are.

CHAPTER 7

Don't Mind the Age Gap

SOME-THING'S GOTTA GIVE

JACK NICHOLSON:
Ahhh, the sweet, uncomplicated satisfaction of the younger woman.

RELEASE DATE
2003

BRIEF DESCRIPTION
When circumstance and complications throw Jack Nicholson and Diane Keaton together, can he overcome his habit of dating young women and see her value — and can she find more in him than just the showy surface?

CAST
Jack Nicholson (Harry Sanborn), Diane Keaton (Erica Barry), Keanu Reeves (Julian Mercer)

LOVER TYPES
Older Man – Younger Woman / Older Woman – Younger Man / Stuck in a Bygone Time

- Youth is not the only attractive attribute for romance.
- Just because you've been doing something for decades does not mean it's still a good idea.
- There's a very interesting thing about passion: It's ageless.

Jack Nicholson: Ahhh, the sweet, uncomplicated satisfaction of the younger woman. That fleeting age when everything just falls right into place. It's magic time. It can render any man, anywhere, absolutely helpless. Some say I'm an expert on the younger woman. Yes... 'cause I've been dating them for over forty years.

Jack Nicholson dates younger women. Period. Right now he's dating Diane Keaton's daughter. Diane is a successful playwright rightfully skeptical about this "romance" with such a large age gap. But when Jack suffers a heart attack during a romantic entanglement with the daughter and they all go to the hospital, Diane herself becomes the object of admiration for young doctor Keanu Reeves. The age gaps loom large in this exploration of what it is we're really after in our search for love. Acceptance, yes. But self-acceptance in a culture that idolizes youth is often difficult, hence the turn to younger partners. Both Jack and Diane are surprised when their attentions turn toward each other. What we can learn here is that it's okay to let go of the age gap pattern. Leap over the gap and be in love with someone your own age if that's where your passions lead you.

SABRINA

AUDREY HEPBURN:
I suppose so.

HUMPHREY BOGART:
Suppose you sing that song again. Slowly.

RELEASE DATE
1954

BRIEF DESCRIPTION
Wealthy older businessman Humphrey Bogart tries to woo young Audrey Hepburn, the chauffeur's daughter, away from his wild younger brother but finds himself falling for her... and her for him, too.

CAST
Humphrey Bogart (Linus Larrabee), Audrey Hepburn (Sabrina Fairchild)

LOVER TYPES
Stuffy and Stodgy / Insecure / Confident / Exuberant / In Love with Someone Else

LOVE LESSONS
- An age gap is often more of a concept than a reality, with tenderness and passion the bridge across the years.

- Just because you think someone's too old/young for you does not mean they really are.
- Pretend you're falling in love and you just might find yourself actually falling in love for real, regardless of age differences.

Humphrey Bogart: How am I ever going to get along in Paris without someone like you? Who'll be there to help me with my French, to turn down the brim of my hat?

Audrey Hepburn: Suppose you meet someone on the boat the very first day out? A perfect stranger.

Humphrey Bogart: I have a better suppose, Sabrina. Suppose I were ten years younger. Suppose you weren't in love with David. Suppose I asked you to... I suppose I'm just talking nonsense.

Audrey Hepburn: I suppose so.

Humphrey Bogart: Suppose you sing that song again. Slowly.

THE STORY

Audrey Hepburn grows up the daughter of the chauffeur of a very wealthy family and nurtures a life-long crush on the wild-child younger son, ignoring his stodgy older brother. But after a stint in Paris the adorable tomboy returns as a sophisticated young woman, determined to pursue her childhood dream, despite the younger son's inability to commit... to anything. Tasked with keeping the chauffeur's daughter away from his younger brother, confirmed bachelor Humphrey Bogart begins his charm offensive. It works all too well and they find themselves falling for each other despite the age gap. It seems love knows no boundaries and if we're smart and want true happiness, we'll ignore them too.

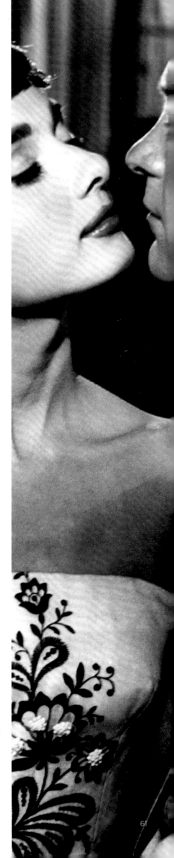

HAROLD AND MAUDE

RUTH GORDON :
Take a chance. Get hurt, even. But play as well as you can.

RELEASE DATE
1971

BRIEF DESCRIPTION
Obsessed with death and destruction, morbid young Harold meets full-of-life verge-of-eighty Maude and starts to see what life and love might really be about.

CAST
Ruth Gordon (Maude), Bud Cort (Harold)

LOVER TYPES
Exuberant / Open-Minded / Full of Life / Wise / Shy / Innocent / Obsessed with Death

LOVE LESSONS
- Grasp life with joy and passion regardless of age.

- Love is about much more than physical appearance.
- An older person most likely knows many things of value to a younger person. If you're older, be generous with your wisdom. If younger, listen and learn — and then enjoy. And if you enjoy it together, good for you.

Ruth Gordon: Vice, virtue. It's best not to be too moral. You cheat yourself out of too much life. Aim above morality. If you apply that to life, then you're bound to live life fully. A lot of people enjoy being dead. But they are not dead, really. They're just backing away from life. Reach out. Take a chance. Get hurt, even. But play as well as you can.

THE STORY

Though the typical age gap is older man–younger woman, sometimes it's the other way around. In this groundbreaking comedy there's more of a chasm than a gap between death-obsessed young Bud Cort and the wise, wisecracking Ruth Gordon, who has enough joie de vivre for both of them. She's old enough to be his grandmother, yet the connection between them is undeniable. Societies dictate the rules of romance and those differ in different times and places. But the heart wants what the heart wants and we're always better off if we admit what it is we really want and are brave enough to go for it where we find it — regardless of what others think appropriate. After all, whose heart is it anyway?

RUMOR HAS IT...

KEVIN COSTNER:

You think I'm too old for you, don't you?

RELEASE DATE
2005

BRIEF DESCRIPTION

It's not just that Kevin Costner has gone after women in three different generations; it's that they're all in the same family. Jennifer Aniston has a hard time dating someone her grandmother had an affair with... and who can blame her?

CAST

Jennifer Aniston (Sarah Huttinger), Kevin Costner (Beau Burroughs)

LOVER TYPES

Womanizer / Insensitive / Rebel / Daring / Competitive / Unsure of Own Commitments

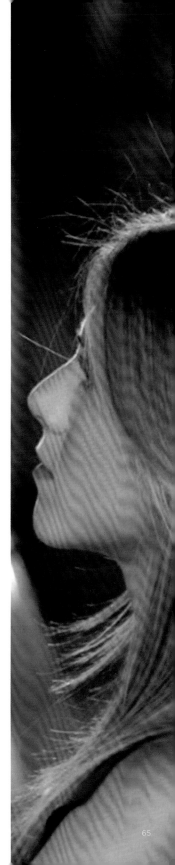

- You don't have to be sensitive about age differences, but do try to be sensitive about others' feelings.
- If someone's old enough to be your parent or young enough to be your child, check first and make sure they're not actually your parent or your child.
- A sense of dignity — in yourself and for others — goes a long way in making that age gap not such a big deal.

QUOTABLE

Kevin Costner: You think I'm too old for you, don't you?

Jennifer Aniston: ... You've slept with my mother and my grandmother.

Kevin Costner: What's your point?

Jennifer Aniston: This is not normal! You are too old for me. I'm very confused.

THE STORY

Some people don't have a problem with age differences in any direction. In fact, Kevin Costner dates the family gene pool in this movie about three generations of women charmed by the same man. No matter the gender or age, sometimes we're drawn to family similarities, perhaps looking for a more perfect version of what attracted us in the first place. When trying to figure out what to do, it often helps to figure out what we really want. If it's breaking taboos or making someone jealous or just stepping outside our own safety zone, we may find better ways to achieve our deeper needs for individual acceptance and personal delight.

CHAPTER 8

Lovers of a Certain Age

THE BEST EXOTIC MARI- GOLD HOTEL

RONALD:

Why must you mock? I just want to feel young again.

2011

BRIEF DESCRIPTION

British retirees Ronald and Celia are birds of a feather: flighty, flirtatious, and always looking for the next conquest, even here in India. Does being older mean they ought to just give up looking for love?

CAST

Ronald Pickup (Norman Cousins), Celia Imrie (Madge Hardcastle)

LOVER TYPES

Ladies' Man / Flirt / Shallow / Vain / Scared of Being Old / Gold Digger / Serial Seducer / Addicted to the Chase

LOVE LESSONS

- Some things change with age, some things don't. Wisdom lies

in figuring out which is which, and which is more important.

- Most of us are searching for the light and the magic. If along the way we can help one another find that, all the better.
- It's not over until it's really all over, so never forget that there are still opportunities for love and romance.

QUOTABLE

Ronald: Why must you mock? I just want to feel young again. To feel needed as much as I need, if only for one night. One wonderful night. Tell me you don't know how that feels.

THE STORY

Ronald has been a ladies' man all his life. Romance and seduction are at the core of his identity and the gauge of his self-worth. Unfortunately, time seems to be catching up and passing him by as his attempts, often misaimed at much younger women, increasingly fail. Traveling to India to a retirement hotel with other Brits his age, he's wandering and lost, trying to find someone to connect with. One of his fellow travelers, herself a huge flirt looking for her next husband, finds him at the local version of a country club, trying to connect with a good-looking older woman. His desperate words strike a warmth of recognition in her heart and she arranges an introduction to that woman, which turns into a wonderful night indeed. And then, into an exciting new romance for Ronald. It seems that desire to feel desire is itself often quite desirable. The magic of love knows no age or gender, status, or ethnicity — the capacity for it lies right within our own hearts and we should never let it go.

SOME-THING'S GOTTA GIVE

RELEASE DATE

2003

BRIEF DESCRIPTION

Jack Nicholson and Diane Keaton are both dating much younger people when they find themselves in a romantic tangle with each other... a surprisingly quite fine one that causes both to reconsider the idea of being with someone their own age.

CAST

Jack Nicholson (Harry Sanborn), Diane Keaton (Erica Barry), Keanu Reeves (Julian Mercer)

LOVER TYPES

Perennial Cradle Robber / Confident Professional / Losing Confidence Because of Age / Daring to Look at Love Differently

KEANU REEVES:

After a heart attack, rule of thumb is: If you can climb a flight of stairs, you can have sex.

- Embracing one's age needn't be limiting at all but can actually be freeing because it's easier to just be who you are without keeping up a front.
- Loosening your grip on what you believe is your "lover type" can put other rich opportunities within your grasp.
- Dignity, joy, and passion are not mutually exclusive.

QUOTABLE

Jack Nicholson: What about Mr. Midnight here… ?

Keanu Reeves: After a heart attack, rule of thumb is: If you can climb a flight of stairs, you can have sex.

THE STORY

Jack Nicholson is sixty-three and only dates women under thirty. Recuperating from a heart attack, Jack is really feeling his age and bemoans being "… old, old, old, old… " Then he starts getting close to a woman his own age, Diane Keaton, who is dating his doctor, the much younger Keanu Reeves. Jack and Diane have an amazing romantic encounter that startles both of them into rethinking what they want. What Jack then finds is that after being with Diane — witty, smart, and beautiful — dating younger women no longer has the appeal it used to for him. What she discovers is that she was right about him and they really should be together. The message? Even with the dignity that can accompany maturity you can still have lots of passion.

MUST LOVE DOGS

CHRISTOPHER PLUMMER:

Maybe if I dance fast enough, I won't remember what I've lost.

RELEASE DATE
2005

BRIEF DESCRIPTION

Widower Christopher Plummer knows no one will ever replace his beloved wife, but figures he might as well be having some fun while he encourages his divorced daughter to engage in the search for real romance.

CAST

Christopher Plummer (Bill), Stockard Channing (Dolly), Diane Lane (Sarah Nolan), John Cusack (Jake)

LOVER TYPES

Still Somewhat in Mourning / Eternal Romantic / Confident / Outspoken / Fun-Loving / Realistic / Courteous / Caring

- Maybe one love-*of*-your-life is enough, and the others can be loves-*in*-your-life.
- With that irreplaceable special love forever up on a pedestal, you can still do some fun dancing around on the ground.
- There are many different types of romances, so if you're willing to explore and experience some others you may really enrich your life.

QUOTABLE

Christopher Plummer: It's different for me. I've had the love of my life and no one else could ever touch that. No one can come close. So I'm just out there, passing the time, tap dancing, if you want the truth. Maybe if I dance fast enough, I won't remember what I've lost.

THE STORY

Christopher Plummer isn't really looking for a new love, but he doesn't mind getting in some fun along the way, including with Stockard Channing, herself very confident, vivacious, and outspoken regardless of her age. He's trying to help his divorced daughter, Diane Lane, find a new love and eventually approves of John Cusack who, like him, is a real romantic as expressed through poetry and movies. It's a difficult thing for many older people to even consider a new relationship, given the changes in their bodies, their family situations, and society's expectations in general. It's especially true if they've already had an amazing romantic love bonding with another person. As the saying goes, "After you've been with the gods, mere mortals cannot compare." But Christopher shows us that maybe they don't have to. You can keep that lost love of your life up on the pedestal and still have rewarding romantic engagements again, just of a different sort.

GRUMPY OLD MEN

RELEASE DATE
1993

BRIEF DESCRIPTION
Rivals for fifty years, Jack Lemmon and Walter Matthau are now fighting over new neighbor Ann-Margret. Things get bleak for Jack, but she may be able to bring some light back into his life.

CAST
Jack Lemmon (John Gustafson), Ann-Margret (Ariel Truax), Walter Matthau (Max Goldman)

LOVER TYPES
Grumpy / Exuberant / Vengeful / Softy Inside / Pessimist / Depressed / Optimist / Peacemaker /

JACK LEMMON:
Ohhh, you don't know a damn thing about me....

- Try not to let a setback in one area of your life spill over into defeatism in others.
- Especially when you're older it's important to be open to and pursue that which can bring you joy.
- Old is a relative term that's constantly being pushed back. Remember when life expectancy was forty? Don't mindlessly accept the label of "old," but do keep enjoying life as much as you possibly can regardless of the calendar.

QUOTABLE

Jack Lemmon: Ohhh, you don't know a damn thing about me....

Ann-Margret: I do too! And I also know the only things in life that you regret, are the risks that you don't take.

THE STORY

Being older doesn't always mean being wiser. Jack Lemmon and Walter Matthau are older and meaner than ever toward each other because Jack stole and married Walter's high school sweetheart. Enter the lovely and lively Ann-Margret and the feud heightens as both men vie for her attentions. Jack has truly fallen for her but, because he's also battling IRS problems, is convinced he can't offer her anything so he breaks up and falls into a depression. It takes Walter's help and urging to get Jack and Ann-Margret back together. It's often difficult to shake off your generation's ideals of what a relationship should be and to dive into the soul of the goal: What is it that really makes you happy? That's what counts.

CHAPTER 9

What Kind of Love Is This?

LOVE ACTUALLY

BILL NIGHY:

... it might be that the people I love is in fact... you.

RELEASE DATE

2003

BRIEF DESCRIPTION

Outrageous rock star Bill Nighy and his soft-spoken manager, Gregor Fisher, are trying to win a Christmas song contest when one of them comes to a startling realization.

CAST

Bill Nighy (Billy Mack), Gregor Fisher (Joe "Chubs")

LOVER TYPES

Arrogant / Spoiled / Narcissistic / Playboy / Devoted / Undemanding / Shy

LOVE LESSONS

- A bromance, even realized late in life, can be a most rewarding relationship.

- Shared history, especially the fun parts, creates a definite sort of love.
- Loyalty is a huge component in love.

Bill Nighy: I realized that Christmas is the time to be with people you love. And, I realized that as dire chance and fateful cock-up would have it, here I am, mid-fifties, and without knowing it I've gone and spent most of my adult life with a chubby employee, and much as it grieves me to say it, it might be that the people I love is in fact... you.

Bill Nighy is an aging rock star angling for a comeback. He makes fun of the Christmas song he's recording as his put-upon manager, Chubs, cringes and tries to get him to take it seriously. To no avail. But Bill's irreverence captures an appreciative audience and his popularity soars again. The night his song wins big he goes off to party at Elton John's. Then not long after he shows up at Chubs's place where Chubs is in for a night alone. Bill declares his realization of love and you can see how touched Chubs is by the heartfelt recognition. It's a bromance here, the kind of love not to be taken lightly but treasured for the special sense of loyalty, shared experiences, and relishing of the "wonderful life" they've had together. When we expand our definition of love, warmth and joy can follow.

THE BIRDCAGE

ROBIN WILLIAMS:
There's only one place in the world I call home, and it's because you're there.

RELEASE DATE
1996

BRIEF DESCRIPTION
Longtime companions Robin Williams and Nathan Lane are both thrilled and concerned about their son's impending marriage and what it will mean to their own relationship.

CAST
Robin Williams (Armand Goldman), Nathan Lane (Albert Goldman)

LOVER TYPES
Drama Queen / Sane One / Complainer / Explainer / Demanding / Illogical / Logical

LOVE LESSONS
- For people used to hiding who they really are (and especially whom they love) being up front and open can bring a real sense of dignity.

- What sometimes looks like fighting is actually fond bickering, another way to fully engage with each other. It's important to be able to tell the difference, though.
- Realization and respect for the longevity of a love relationship can strengthen it and bring even more joy.

QUOTABLE

Robin Williams: What a pain in the ass you are. And it's true: you're not young, you're not new, and you do make people laugh. And me? I'm still with you because you make me laugh.... There. We're partners now. You own half of my life and I own half of your life. I'm fifty years old. There's only one place in the world I call home, and it's because you're there. So take it. What difference does it make if I say you can stay or if you say I can stay?

THE STORY

Robin Williams is a gay cabaret owner and his longtime lover and companion is Nathan Lane, a drag-queen diva. The son they raised (product of Robin's one-night fling with Christine Baranski) is about to marry the daughter of a very conservative senator, so their unconventional partnership is under scrutiny. After nervous pressure from Nathan, Robin agrees to a palimony arrangement and lets him know about it with a declaration of love in keeping with their years of verbal sparring. Regardless of societal or legal formulas, real love knows no boundaries. And when the stresses that wear on love arise, a sense of humor can go a long way to keeping people together.

CHASING AMY

JOEY LAUREN ADAMS:
I feel justified lying in your arms, 'cause I got here on my own terms.

RELEASE DATE
1997

BRIEF DESCRIPTION
Ben Affleck falls for Joey Lauren Adams, who he discovers is a lesbian; Joey falls for him in spite of that. How can this possibly work out?

CAST
Ben Affleck (Holden McNeil), Joey Lauren Adams (Alyssa Jones)

LOVER TYPES
Exploring Gender Identity / On the Platonic Border

LOVE LESSONS
- A willingness to cross and break boundaries can lead to the discovery of ever richer types of love.

- Love is love regardless of gender identity, and once you're okay with that, not much else matters.
- The foundation of a good relationship — no matter the sexual inclinations — is mutual respect and friendship.

Joey Lauren Adams: I'm not with you because of what family, society, life tried to instill in me from day one. The way the world is, how seldom it is that you meet that one person who just gets you — it's so rare. ... And to cut oneself off from finding that person, to immediately halve your options by eliminating the possibility of finding that one person within your own gender, that just seemed stupid to me. So I didn't. But then you came along. ... And while I was falling for you I put a ceiling on that, because you were a guy. Until I remembered why I opened the door to women in the first place: to not limit the likelihood of finding that one person who'd complement me so completely. ... I feel justified lying in your arms, 'cause I got here on my own terms, and I have no question there was someplace I didn't look. And for me that makes all the difference.

THE STORY

In this smart, irreverent rom-com Ben Affleck is a comic book creator who falls for Joey Lauren Adams, only to discover to his dismay that she is a lesbian. They become fast friends, though, and both feel something more developing between them. Ben's creative partner, Jason Lee, becomes rather jealous of his time with Joey. Then Ben is confronted with some of Joey's past, including some rather racy sexual escapades. Joey explains, in a profoundly insightful way for a rom-com, about her search for her own identity and what she really wants in a romantic relationship. The friendship is solid, the romantic love is undeniable, and good for them — they do end up together. As more people explore the gender and sexuality spectrums it behooves us all to remember that what's important is the passionate connection between two hearts and souls, regardless of the bodies they inhabit.

TO WONG FU, THANKS FOR EVERY-THING! JULIE NEWMAR

STOCKARD CHANNING:
I think of you as an angel.

RELEASE DATE
1995

BRIEF DESCRIPTION
Drag queen Patrick Swayze befriends small-town housewife Stockard Channing and in an act of chivalrous love, helps free her from her abusive husband.

CAST
Patrick Swayze (Vida), Stockard Channing (Carol Ann), Wesley Snipes (Noxeema), John Leguizamo (Chi-Chi)

LOVER TYPES
Strong / Daring / Protective / Fun-Loving / Supportive / Inspiring / Chivalrous / Abused / Fearful / Insecure / Hopeful

- Being loved by someone who finds us worthy of love can help us rise up to their hopes and expectations for us, even if there isn't any physical intimacy.
- The essence of love is always wanting the best for the other person, even if they sometimes drive you wacky.
- Your own love for life can enliven and inspire others so do share it; you never know what lives you'll change.

QUOTABLE

Stockard Channing: Vida, I do not think of you as a man and I do not think of you as a woman. I think of you as an angel.
Patrick Swayze: I think that's healthy!

THE STORY

Three macho actors playing drag queens temporarily stuck in small-town America? It could be funny. It could be moving. It could be good. Rest assured, it's all three. Patrick Swayze and Wesley Snipes have just won a contest to go to Hollywood and are driving across the country mentoring a young drag princess, John Leguizamo. Their car breaks down and while waiting for repairs they meet Stockard Channing, the abused wife of one of the town bigots. Patrick and she form a friendship based on understanding and acceptance, and he even gives Stockard's abusive husband a taste of his own medicine. Stockard gains courage and self-respect because of how Patrick, Wesley, and John portray and support her and the other women in the town — strong, feminine, and feisty while also being courageous and chivalrous. Part of real love is affording the other person their dignity. When Stockard thanks Patrick for what he has done for her she is expressing a very real love. How can we not love those who bravely help us become more of who we really are and who give us the courage to move forward?

CHAPTER 10

Family Foibles

BRIDE & PREJUDICE

LALITA:

Mother thinks that any single man with big bucks is shopping for a wife.

RELEASE DATE

2004

BRIEF DESCRIPTION

Aishwarya Rai Bachchan's eccentric family and Martin Henderson's snobby family threaten to keep them apart in spite of their growing attraction.

CAST

Aishwarya Rai Bachchan (Lalita Bakshi), Martin Henderson (William Darcy)

LOVER TYPES

Snobby / Remote / Skeptical / Loyal / Kind / Wild / Rebellious / Geeky / Shy

LOVE LESSONS

- Every family has a wide range of characters that often must be dealt with;

honesty and firmness is usually the best way to handle them.

- Families can absorb the individual so you often have to take a stand to be yourself and have your own life — and love.
- Different cultures approach it different ways, but strong romantic attraction can overcome barriers of tradition and family expectations.

QUOTABLE

Lalita: Mother thinks that any single man with big bucks is shopping for a wife.

THE STORY

Cultures clash, classes clash... what can lovers from either side of those great divides do? Set *Pride and Prejudice* in tradition-bound contemporary India and watch the saris and the Savile Row suits fly. All the characters from the original are here, but with really fun Bollywood-style singing and dancing. Like Eliza Bennet in the original, Aishwarya Rai Bachchan loves her patient father, worrying mother, calm older sister, and her two younger sisters — one wild and the other artistically eclectic, to be kind about it. Their eccentricities pose problems for her reluctant but growing attraction to American hotel heir Martin Henderson, Mr. Darcy. Martin's family and friends aren't too thrilled by the prospects of their getting together either. Yet as in Jane Austen's original story, in spite of the dilemmas and setbacks imposed by society and family, the lovers cross the great divides, and passion, dignity, and true love win the day.

EASY VIRTUE

JESSICA BIEL:
I'm sorry. I can't change.

RELEASE DATE
2008

BRIEF DESCRIPTION

Free-spirited American Jessica Biel marries into a stuffy English family headed by bossy mother Kristin Scott Thomas and shell-shocked father Colin Firth. Her marriage to younger man Ben Barnes is under assault by tradition and family prejudices.

CAST

Jessica Biel (Larita Whittaker), Colin Firth (Mr. Whittaker), Kristin Scott Thomas (Veronica Whittaker), Ben Barnes (John Whittaker)

LOVER TYPES

Independent / Daring / Adventurous / Passionate / Weak-Willed / Immature / Jealous / Territorial / Wounded / Sardonic / Ditzy / Delusional

- It's one thing to try to blend in a bit à la "When in Rome" but not when it compromises your own integrity.
- Families can band together against what they feel is an outsider; when that happens it's probably wise to get out before it gets worse.
- In family conflicts, keep your intuition working and you may find an ally where you least expect it.

QUOTABLE

Jessica Biel: I'm sorry. I can't change. Not for you, not for anybody, not anymore.

THE STORY

American race car driver Jessica Biel has just married young English aristocrat Ben Barnes. They arrive at Ben's family's country estate, where Jessica is coolly received by Ben's snobby mother, Kristin Scott Thomas. His two ditzy sisters both struggle with finding love and vacillate between adoring Jessica and being appalled by her. The shell-shocked father, Colin Firth, left part of his soul in the trenches of World War I. In this Noel Coward story with his ever-witty dialogue, free-spirited Jessica is increasingly confined by the family's stodgy traditions and expectations of how she should behave. Eventually even Ben tries to rein her in but Jessica, still healing from her own tragic love-loss, refuses to stifle herself. Her joie de vivre helps Ben's father break away too, and Jessica and Colin depart together for unknown adventures. Sometimes when the parts don't seem to fit and you're told to compromise your integrity, it's a sign that you should quit while you're ahead and drive back onto the path of joy.

THE BIRD-CAGE

GENE HACKMAN:
I don't want to be the only girl not dancing!

RELEASE DATE
1996

BRIEF DESCRIPTION

Ultraconservative senator Gene Hackman is at first shocked to discover his daughter's fiancé's parents are a gay couple. But when they help him out of a potentially politically damaging jam by dressing him up as a drag queen... well, dancing awhile in the other person's high heels goes a long way toward understanding.

CAST

Gene Hackman (Senator Kevin Keeley), Calista Flockhart (Barbara Keeley), Robin Williams (Armand Goldman), Nathan Lane (Albert Goldman)

Repressed / Prejudiced / Fearful / Proud /
Domineering / Defiant / Fun-Loving

LOVE LESSONS
- Every family has secrets; some are just more
  entertaining than others.
- The desire for acknowledgment,
  understanding, and respect is universal; find
  that and the differences between people fade.
- Love for the children can override differences
  among the adults.

QUOTABLE

Gene Hackman: Don't leave me. Don't leave me
here. I don't want to be the only girl not dancing!
No one will dance with me. I think it's this dress. I
told them white would make me look fat.

THE STORY

Gay cabaret owner Robin Williams and his drag
queen companion, Nathan Lane, face a dilemma
when the son they raised together becomes
engaged to the daughter of conservative US
senator Gene Hackman and it's time for the
families to meet. Though gay marriage is now
legal in many places, the concept of winning
the other family's approval can still be quite
a challenge. In this movie the gay couple first
puts on a front for the straight family but that
falls to pieces. Then as Senator Hackman is
pursued by the press and needs to escape,
Robin and Nathan offer him the perfect disguise
— as a drag queen. Living a moment in the
other person's life goes a long way toward
understanding and acceptance. Would that it
were always as much fun as in this movie.

RUMOR HAS IT...

RELEASE DATE

2005

BRIEF DESCRIPTION

Jennifer Aniston's family history is a bit complicated: Her grandmother and her mother were both lovers of Kevin Kostner and now she's being drawn under his spell. With a background like that, what's a girl to do?

CAST

Jennifer Aniston (Sarah Huttinger), Kevin Kostner (Beau Burroughs), Shirley MacLaine (Katharine Richelieu), Richard Jenkins (Earl Huttinger)

LOVER TYPES

Womanizer / Insensitive / Rebel / Daring / Competitive / Unsure of Own Commitments / Accepting

JENNIFER ANISTON:

Maybe every girl in my family has to sleep with you.

- Competition is common between relatives of the same gender; be careful not to get caught up in that drama.
- We actually can learn from other people's mistakes.
- Don't get locked into family tradition; make your own decisions and have your own experiences.

QUOTABLE

Jennifer Aniston: Obviously, last night was some rite of passage. Maybe every girl in my family has to sleep with you.

Kevin Costner: I don't know if they have to, but they certainly have.

THE STORY

Jennifer Aniston is engaged to Mark Ruffalo and takes him to meet her family, where he learns they were the inspiration for the movie *The Graduate*. Her deceased mother was the model for Elaine and her very lively grandmother Shirley MacLaine was the infamous Mrs. Robinson, who still has a wry and challenging sense of humor. Enter Kevin Costner as the iconic Ben and everyone's got a generational snarl on their hands. Seriously, who dates an entire gene pool? And what about Kevin and Jennifer? Lovers? Father and daughter? Way too confusing. Mark throws up his hands and leaves. Jennifer, at first horrified she might have slept with her father, is relieved to learn he's sterile. She also comes to realize she really loves Mark and they reunite, on the condition that any daughter of theirs doesn't go near Ben. There's often a lot of competition between family members and sometimes it gets way, way out of hand. It takes clear eyes and a wise head to see and avoid the snares too often inherent in those ties that bind.

SECTION THREE

"The most enduring loves are not the ones we choose, but those we are powerless to resist."

FRANK DEFORD, *sportswriter and novelist*

CHAPTER 11

Crazy Love! Is It Worth It?

BRIDGET JONES'S DIARY

RENÉE ZELLWEGER:
Will especially stop fantasizing about a particular person who embodies all these things.

RELEASE DATE
2001

BRIEF DESCRIPTION
Renée Zellweger knows she's crazy and is trying to reform. She's not very successful but two men want her anyway. One is a bad-boy cad and the other a respectable, sensible man — and both are exceptionally attractive. Can she possibly make the best decision for herself?

CAST
Renée Zellweger (Bridget Jones), Colin Firth (Mark Darcy), Hugh Grant (Daniel Cleaver)

LOVER TYPES
Neurotic / Fun-Loving / Insecure / Self-Critical / Cad / Narcissist / Sedate / Perceptive

- Self-criticism can keep us so focused on ourselves we miss what other people think and feel about us.
- There's a lot of merit in the old saying, "When casting out demons beware you don't cast out the best part of yourself."
- Enthusiasm for life is a most attractive characteristic... as long as you don't totally overdo it.

QUOTABLE

Renée Zellweger: Resolution number one: obviously will lose twenty pounds. Equally important, will find nice sensible boyfriend and not continue to form romantic attachments to alcoholics, workaholics, peeping toms, megalomaniacs, emotional fuckwits, or perverts. Will especially stop fantasizing about a particular person who embodies all these things.

THE STORY

Renée Zellweger is, by her own admission, crazy. She has very little discipline or self-control. She is easily led astray by the lure of personal excess, partying, and bad boys. Yet she is possessed by the need to clean up her act, all of which will be documented in her diary. It doesn't go all that well. Crazily drawn to her bounder of a boss, Hugh Grant, she is also interested in her childhood friend Colin Firth, who is now a respectable attorney. What's a girl to do? Fortunately for her, Colin Firth sees through her craziness and actually wants to seriously date her... and possibly more. What she has to do first is accept herself as she is. He's able to do that; she has to work on it. Really though, think about it, what's crazy for one person is just eccentric for another.

AS GOOD AS IT GETS

RELEASE DATE
1997

BRIEF DESCRIPTION
Novelist Jack Nicholson is really hard to tolerate, much less like. Waitress Helen Hunt deals with him every day and, in spite of both himself and herself, begins to see more in him than the grumpy guy with OCD. Will that be enough for him to start to change?

CAST
Jack Nicholson (Melvin Udall), Helen Hunt (Carol Connelly)

LOVER TYPES
Obsessive-Compulsive / Misanthrope / Prickly / Self-Protective / Tolerant / Kind

HELEN HUNT:

Do you have any control over how creepy you allow yourself to get?

- You can tell a lot about a person by the way they treat animals and innocents.
- Beneath that prickly exterior may well beat a kind heart... if only you can muster the patience to look for it.
- Everyone has ghosts and demons. Sometimes in some people, they mask what Abraham Lincoln called "the better angels of our nature." Nurture the angels.

QUOTABLE

Helen Hunt: Do you have any control over how creepy you allow yourself to get?

THE STORY

Jack Nicholson is a novelist with OCD who insists on sitting at waitress Helen Hunt's booth and being served certain foods a certain way, eating with his own plastic utensils. She's tolerant of him but has her own problems with her asthmatic son. Jack's also a misanthrope and just pretty much doesn't like anyone. When his neighbor Greg Kinnear gets robbed and mugged, Jack is handed custody of Greg's dog, who unlike any humans, takes a liking to the curmudgeon. Even on a road trip helping Greg to reunite with his family, Helen finds a great many of Jack's actions deplorable. Though he eventually helps out with her son's medical situation, it takes a lot of patience for Helen to even consider approaching the craziness of loving this man. But his winning comment, which is at the core of all chivalric transformative love, is "You make me want to be a better man." Just maybe, beneath all that crazy, there might be a real person worth loving. If you have any sense of that at all in your relationship, it's probably worth checking out.

BREAKFAST AT TIFFANY'S

AUDREY HEPBURN:
You know those days when you get the mean reds?

GEORGE PEPPARD:
The mean reds, you mean like the blues?

RELEASE DATE
1961

BRIEF DESCRIPTION
Audrey Hepburn's making her way in New York by being pretty, flighty, and fun. But inside, she often feels lost and depressed. Her handsome new neighbor George Peppard is pretty much the same. Can these two searching souls help each other?

CAST
Audrey Hepburn (Holly Golightly), George Peppard (Paul Varjak)

LOVER TYPES
Flighty / Moody / Self-Destructive / Social Climber / Frustrated Artiste / Sex-for-Money

- The search for love and self-acceptance can become a frenzied swirl downward if you're not careful.
- Everyone needs a "safe" place, person, or idea where you can go to refocus and regain a sense of their true self.
- Dare to go through and then past the crazy and you may well find great value.

Audrey Hepburn: You know those days when you get the mean reds?

George Peppard: The mean reds, you mean like the blues?

Audrey Hepburn: No. The blues are because you're getting fat and maybe it's been raining too long, you're just sad, that's all. The mean reds are horrible. Suddenly you're afraid and you don't know what you're afraid of. Do you ever get that feeling?

George Peppard: Sure.

Audrey Hepburn: Well, when I get it the only thing that does any good is to jump in a cab and go to Tiffany's. Calms me down right away. The quietness and the proud look of it; nothing very bad could happen to you there. If I could find a real-life place that'd make me feel like Tiffany's, then — then I'd buy some furniture and give the cat a name!

Mood swings can make most of us seem pretty crazy at times. New York party girl Audrey Hepburn (transplanted from small-town Texas) is subject to serious mood swings as she tries to make her way up the ladder of success with her looks being her most valuable asset. Yet she feels comfortable confessing to her friend George Peppard, who is himself a writer (and a kept man depending on his own good looks for any success so far) and subject to his own moodiness. The friendship between these two misfits grows in part because both of them are flying in the face of what is deemed normal. Sometimes when you feel nobody really understands you, finding someone who really does seem to understand you can hasten the steps from like to love. One good thing about people who are slightly crazy but not so crazy as to hurt themselves and others? They can be an awful lot of fun!

THE APRIL FOOLS

JACK LEMMON:

I'm not a frog now. I'm a prince. But I was a frog.

RELEASE DATE

1969

BRIEF DESCRIPTION

Both stuck in unhappy marriages, Jack Lemmon and Catherine Deneuve meet and quickly fall inappropriately in love and decide to run away together. Crazy, huh? Now how to break away from their seemingly successful but hollow lives...

CAST

Jack Lemmon (Howard Brubaker), Catherine Deneuve (Catherine Gunther)

LOVER TYPES

Unhappily Married / Unfulfilled Professionally / Trophy Wife / Yearning for Love / Desperate to Be Real

- As long as you're living other people's ideas about how you should be, you'll never really be you.
- The things you most regret are not the things you did but the things you did not do.
- Just go for it!

QUOTABLE

Jack Lemmon: You don't understand. It was nothing like that. See, she's... she's a princess and I'm a frog who got changed into a prince.
Boss: That's enough, Brubaker....
Jack Lemmon: But then I got changed into a frog until her kiss.
Boss: Brubaker, you're not a frog.
Jack Lemmon: I'm not a frog now. I'm a prince. But I was a frog.
Boss: Brubaker. You need some rest. You also need to consult a doctor. Either a psychiatrist... or a veterinarian.

THE STORY

Jack Lemmon and Catherine Deneuve, both married to other people, have just met and must be crazy to take up with each other, but both are in unfulfilling marriages: He's unappreciated and she's a lonely trophy wife. In this sophisticated '60s psychedelic rom-com, a man who nobody really gets is finally "seen" by a lovely, sensitive woman (think how the Na'vi say "I see you" in *Avatar*) and he comes alive. They both must be crazy to even get together in the first place, much less decide to run off to Paris together, but they are inspired by an older, very happy couple still very much in love after thirty-five years. Everyone else tells them they're crazy. But then, most of the rest of the people in this story are stuck in roles and responsibilities that bind them and are also crazy in some way too. Often we have to be just a little bit crazy ourselves to see past the front most people put up, or the assumptions other people place on us. Jack and Catherine can encourage us to be crazy enough to explore what we really want and brave enough to go for it.

CHAPTER 12

A Cynic? (Or Just a Wounded Romantic?)

27 DRESSES

2008

BRIEF DESCRIPTION

Katherine Heigl's always doing things for other people, even when it means a loss for her. James Marsden is totally the opposite. Maybe a dose of his self-reliance could be good for her. Maybe.

CAST

Katherine Heigl (Jane), James Marsden (Kevin)

LOVER TYPES

Accommodating / Selfless / People Pleaser / Distant / Disillusioned / Cynical / Cranky

LOVE LESSONS

- There's a difference between being good and being nice. If

KATHERINE HEIGL:

Kevin, I've been waiting my whole life for the right guy to come along and then you showed up.

you're too nice to others you're most likely not being good to yourself.

- Sometimes arguing can be refreshing — at least there's an inherent sense of equality and often empowerment in being in the same ring together.
- That person who points out your weaknesses may be doing you a favor and may have your best interest at heart.

QUOTABLE

Katherine Heigl: Kevin, I've been waiting my whole life for the right guy to come along and then you showed up. And you are nothing like the man I imagined. You're cynical and cranky and impossible. But the truth is, fighting with you is the best thing that's ever happened to me. And I think there's a very good chance that I'm falling in love with you.

THE STORY

Katherine Heigl is always doing things for other people, like being a bridesmaid twenty-seven times. James Marsden is a journalist who writes romantically about weddings under a pseudonym but is personally very cynical about what he perceives: a delusional, hypocritical spectacle. Sensing a good story in Katherine, he spends time with her to get more material, and sees that her manipulative sister has snatched up the boss Katherine holds a crush on. Beginning to actually like Katherine, he tries to stop the exposé but it runs anyway and she feels very betrayed. And yet... there is that undeniably growing attraction between them which, once they act on it, changes everything. James tells Katherine she deserves more than she has been settling for. His truthful words shake her world and Katherine becomes more realistic about romance and what she needs, which simultaneously allows her to experience more love — even if it is with a cynical man. A man who cares about her feelings. Who wants the best for her. Maybe he is really a romantic after all. Like the saying goes, "Actions speak louder than words."

THE UGLY TRUTH

GERARD BUTLER:
Women would have us believe that they are the victims; that we break their hearts for sport. That's crap.

RELEASE DATE
2009

BRIEF DESCRIPTION
Cynic Gerard Butler and idealist Katherine Heigl have competing TV talk shows. Whose view of romance is right? How many hearts will get broken in this fight? Or just maybe there's something to that old saying "Opposites attract."

CAST
Katherine Heigl (Abby), Gerard Butler (Mike)

LOVER TYPES
Cynical / Brutally Honest / Disillusioned / Insistently Romantic

- The romantic games people play are predictable and manipulable. Do you really want to go there?
- There's often a valuable purity in the cynic's brutally honest observations, if you take time to really listen and look deeper.
- People far apart on the spectrum of romance often find the sparks of conflict turn into sparks of attraction, and more.

QUOTABLE

Gerard Butler: Let me tell you something about women. Women would have us believe that they are the victims; that we break their hearts for sport. That's crap. They say they want romance, they say they want true love, but all they want is a checklist. Is he perfect? Is he handsome? Is he a doctor? Money over substance, looks over soul, polished over principles. No gesture, no matter how real or romantic, will ever compensate for a really impressive list of credentials.

THE STORY

Gerard Butler has a popular talk show giving "truthful" and not very pretty advice about relationships. Katherine Heigl's TV show features an idealistic romantic approach but her ratings are dropping. They're thrown together by her producers and Gerard tosses down the challenge that he can advise her how to get the man she's fallen for to fall for her. If it fails, he'll leave her show. She agrees, plays all the games Gerard suggests, and sure enough, she wins the guy. Over drinks one night Gerard finally admits that his dark attitude about love was born of shattered idealism and a series of heartbreaks. Then they dance and oh, there is definitely some romance going on there, including a very steamy kiss. Katherine undergoes her own revelations: This new guy is only after who she is pretending to be. She wants truthful love. And wouldn't you know it, that's going to be with the wounded romantic, formerly cynical Gerard. Sometimes the real truth isn't ugly at all — once we're willing to face it.

DOWN WITH LOVE

RELEASE DATE
2003

BRIEF DESCRIPTION
Renée Zellweger and Ewan McGregor are both pretending to be people they're not in order to get one over on the other. She's a romantic masquerading as a cynic and he's just the opposite. How long can this game go on before true feelings start to grow and emerge?

CAST
Renée Zellweger (Barbara Novak), Ewan McGregor (Catcher Block)

LOVER TYPES
Cynical / Disappointed / Self-Protective / Self-Sufficient / Playboy / Playgirl / Masquerader

LOVE LESSONS

- Cynicism can be a shield and a bandage for a broken heart, so you might want to look beyond the cynicism to see if that's the case.
- The differences between genders fall away the closer you get to the heart of what everybody deep down really wants from love.
- The freer we all become from societal expectations about behaviors and roles the richer our romances can be.

QUOTABLE

Renée Zellweger: I've become a Down with Love girl, level three. I don't want love, and I don't want you.

THE STORY

How about two cynics in the same movie going against each other? In this catchy spoof on Doris Day – Rock Hudson films, Renée Zellweger is a celebrity author whose book urges girls not to fall in love but be like guys and just have sex for fun. Oh, and don't worry about that marriage thing either. Magazine writer and man-about-town Ewan McGregor is one of those guys and he's determined to get a story exposing Renée as really just like all women — wanting love and commitment. As they each try to catch the other out, he starts falling in love with her and she keeps him at arm's length until — in a clash of wills they peel away the layers of cynicism until all that's left is love. Keeping in mind that cynicism is often a shield and a bandage for a wounded heart can inspire us to search beneath it for that passion just waiting to be reignited.

IT HAPPENED ONE NIGHT

CLAUDETTE COLBERT:

It seems to me you could make some girl wonderfully happy.

RELEASE DATE
1934

BRIEF DESCRIPTION

Claudette Colbert is running away to marry someone her millionaire dad disapproves of while reporter Clark Gable is looking for a good story (he's given up looking for a good woman). On a road trip masquerading as husband and wife they start seeing the results of "fake it till you make it." Will integrity or romance win the day? Must they be in conflict?

CAST

Claudette Colbert (Ellie Andrews), Clark Gable (Peter Warne)

LOVER TYPES

Cynical / Spoiled / Rebellious / No Longer Looking / World-Weary

LOVE LESSONS

- Before getting into a relationship or situation as serious as marriage, carefully examine your motives.
- If you already have an idea what you're looking for you're more likely to find it.
- Two wrongs don't make a right, but two cynics can kindle a romance.

QUOTABLE

Claudette Colbert: It seems to me you could make some girl wonderfully happy.

Clark Gable: Sure... if I could ever meet the right sort of girl. Aw, where you gonna find her? Somebody that's real. Somebody that's alive. They don't come that way anymore. Have I ever thought about it? I've even been sucker enough to make plans. You know, I saw an island in the Pacific once. I've never been able to forget it. That's where I'd like to take her. She'd have to be the sort of a girl who'd... well, who'd jump in the surf with me and love it as much as I did. You know, nights when you and the moon and the water all become one. You feel you're part of something big and marvelous. That's the only place to live... where the stars are so close over your head you feel you could reach up and stir them around. Certainly, I've been thinking about it. Boy, if I could ever find a girl who was hungry for those things...

THE STORY

This classic rom-com pits out-of-work reporter Clark Gable against runaway heiress Claudette Colbert, who's trying to reunite with a gold digger her father disapproves of. They're both rather cynical, these two. As a journalist, he's covered the less savory aspects of humanity and sees her as just a spoiled rich kid. She doesn't have much use for idealism and mainly just wants to rebel against her controlling dad. Neither Clark nor Claudette approve of each other but she agrees to give him an exclusive story if he'll help her get to her fiancé. As can happen on those unpredictable throw-you-together road trips, in between the clever banter and the jibes, they start to reveal more of themselves. Before too long they've fallen in love and even have to pretend to be married to get a motel room. Now that's a recipe for transformation of a relationship. This particular cynical guy, however, is honorable and he firmly but certainly deflects her declaration of love. It's an odd thing but true that some cynics also have a lot of integrity: They see the truth and know what's really important in life. We all might learn something from those kind of cynics. Oh, and Clark's integrity eventually wins him the girl.

CHAPTER 13

I Hate You, I Love You

THE PRO-POSAL

RYAN REYNOLDS:
Three days ago, I loathed you.

RELEASE DATE
2009

BRIEF DESCRIPTION
Bossy Sandra Bullock hates to ask her assistant, Ryan Reynolds, to marry her and he hates to accept, but she needs a visa to stay in the country and he wants a promotion.

CAST
Sandra Bullock (Margaret Tate), Ryan Reynolds (Andrew Paxton)

LOVER TYPES
Pushy / Narcissist / Proud / Disdainful / Compromised / Reluctant / Vulnerable / Surprised

LOVE LESSONS
● Hate... love... both are very strong emotions often on the flip side of each other and a little more

understanding is a fine way to flip that switch from hate to love.

- Pride goeth before a great fall to the knees — if you're lucky in love.
- Sometimes when you get what you asked for it turns out to be something far more wonderful than you realized you were asking for in the first place.

Ryan Reynolds: Three days ago, I loathed you. I used to dream about you getting hit by a cab. Or poisoned. ...Things changed when we kissed. And when you told me about your tattoo. Even when you checked me out when we were naked. But I didn't realize any of this, until I was standing alone... in a barn... wifeless. Now, you could imagine my disappointment when it suddenly dawned on me that the woman I love is about to be kicked out of the country. So Margaret, marry me — because I'd like to date you.

THE STORY

Ryan Reynolds is the beleaguered assistant to witchy publishing boss Sandra Bullock, whose visa is about to expire. If she doesn't marry an American she'll have to return to Canada. She bribes Ryan to marry her in return for a promotion, plus she'll publish a book he's been pushing. It's a loathsome thing, but he is an ambitious young man. Meeting his family, she discovers more about him than he's willing to tell, but she opens up about being alone and missing her own family. In trying to learn enough about each other to convince the immigration officer it's a real marriage, both begin to change their opinions about each other. Proposals are flying all over the place and the formerly high-handed boss even gets down on her knees on a New York sidewalk to propose to him. The things that throw us together can feel uncomfortable at first, but a little understanding goes a long way. The thing about hate and love is that they are both very intense emotions and if you can just flip that switch from "hate you" to "love you"... oh my!

ROMANC- ING THE STONE

RELEASE DATE
1984

BRIEF DESCRIPTION
Romance writer Kathleen Turner is on a rescue mission and falls in with treasure hunter Michael Douglas, who hates being saddled with such a softy but hopes to claim the ransom prize for himself.

CAST
Kathleen Turner (Joan Wilder), Michael Douglas (Jack T. Colton)

LOVER TYPES
Hopeless Romantic / Unworldly / Meek / Adventurous / Lone Wolf / World-Weary /

LOVE LESSONS
- What you see when you first meet tells you very little about what a person can actually become.

MICHAEL DOUGLAS:
What did you do, wake up this morning and say, "Today, I'm going to ruin a man's life?"

- That initial feeling of repulsion may be an early warning sign that you may well get tangled up with that person in a way that'll change your life.
- People do affect and often become more like each other the more time they spend together — especially if they're falling in love.

Michael Douglas: What did you do, wake up this morning and say, "Today, I'm going to ruin a man's life?"

THE STORY

When they first meet in Colombia, adventurer Michael Douglas sees romance novelist Kathleen Turner as nothing but trouble. She's there to ransom her sister with a treasure map but he's a treasure hunter himself so off they go, pursued by all sorts of bad guys, kidnappers, and drug lords. He's frustrated being saddled with her: She's too soft, she's too idealistic, she's — quite famous down there as it turns out. Glimpsing the value of her writer's reputation, Michael begins to view her differently. And all the while, she's stepping more and more into a sense of adventure and courage. Some acts of bravery and bravado, some sexy dancing, plus a night of passion... well, Michael now has a much different feeling toward Kathleen. What brings us together may seem repellent at first but what keeps us together often springs out of those very first situations. Getting a different perspective on things can often shift everything. It worked well for these two, and who couldn't use a huge emerald or a sleek sailboat along with a new love?

YOU'VE GOT MAIL

TOM HANKS:

How can you forgive this guy for standing you up and not forgive me for this tiny little thing of... of putting you out of business?

RELEASE DATE
1998

BRIEF DESCRIPTION
Meg Ryan hates Tom Hanks because he shut down her small bookstore, but online behind other names they're falling in love. Can they cross that hate/love divide?

CAST
Tom Hanks (Joe Fox), Meg Ryan (Kathleen Kelly)

LOVER TYPES
Vulnerable / Shy / Ambitious / Ruthless / Wounded / Apologetic

LOVE LESSONS
- We all hide behind many masks; be sure to look behind some of them before you reject someone outright.

- When someone shows you their vulnerable self and you like what you see, help bring that more to the fore and honor it.
- Don't let the outer world ruin your inner world.

Tom Hanks: And you and I would have never been at war. And the only thing we'd fight about would be which video to rent on a Saturday night.

Meg Ryan: Well, who fights about that?

Tom Hanks: Well, some people. Not us.

Meg Ryan: We would never.

Tom Hanks: If only.

Meg Ryan: I gotta go.

Tom Hanks: Well, let me ask you something. How can you forgive this guy for standing you up and not forgive me for this tiny little thing of... of putting you out of business?

[*Meg starts to cry*]

Tom Hanks: Oh, how I wish you would.

Seriously, how could you not hate someone who just destroyed your beloved family business? Tom Hanks's big bookstore chain has just edged out Meg Ryan's small boutique bookstore. Okay, that's bad enough. But there are multiple relationships going on here as they start to fall for each other in person while, unbeknownst to either of them, they are the very same people they've both fallen for online behind hidden identities. This layer cake is spiced through and through with hate you / love you tensions that make it both poignant and funny. One thing's for sure, you'll probably not ever know everything about anybody, but keeping your eyes and your heart open can often transport you from one side of that hate/love divide to the other.

GRUMPIER OLD MEN

WALTER MATTHAU:
[singing] *I just met a girl named Maria!*

RELEASE DATE
1995

BRIEF DESCRIPTION
Sophia Loren wants to turn the local bait shop into a fancy restaurant and Walter Matthau froths with hatred for the beautiful woman who's destroying his fishing world... until he discovers she likes to fish, too. Hmmm...

CAST
Sophia Loren (Maria Sophia Coletta Ragetti), Walter Matthau (Max Goldman), Ann-Margret (Ariel Gustafson), Jack Lemmon (John Gustafson)

LOVER TYPES
Angry / Grumpy / Independent / Dynamic / Competitive / Sporting / Dedicated to Their Passion

- Shared passion for a thing or activity can help overcome conflicts.
- Differences of opinion can be healthy for a relationship if they keep things interesting and are expressed with respect.
- Once we're willing to change, we can grow into someone we may like a whole lot better.

QUOTABLE

Walter Matthau: [singing] I just met a girl named Maria! And now I plainly see, she's not the bitch I thought she would be!

THE STORY

There's a whole lot of hating going on in this sequel to the popular *Grumpy Old Men*, including fishing rivalries and unresolved family drama among at least three of the couples. Who could hate the lovely Sophia Loren? Walter Matthau does because she's intent on turning the local bait shop into a fancy Italian restaurant. Even though at odds about that, Walter and Sophia share a love of fishing so the chasm between their positions begins to narrow. By the end of the misunderstandings, sparring, reassessments, and apologies something resembling peace starts to reign. So much of what we enjoy in drama is watching characters change and grow; there's plenty of it here. One thing about a good argument: It does get the blood up. And as the saying goes, there's a certain piquancy to "make-up love."

CHAPTER 14

Commitment Issues? What Commitment Issues?

ANNIE HALL

WOODY ALLEN:
... it's like a free-floating life raft that we know we're not married.

RELEASE DATE
1977

BRIEF DESCRIPTION
Woody Allen's giving Diane Keaton very mixed messages: He wants her but he's afraid to become tied down and lost in a relationship so he simultaneously keeps his distance.

CAST
Woody Allen (Alvy Singer), Diane Keaton (Annie Hall)

LOVER TYPES
Insecure / Push-Pull / Confused / Disappointed / Fearful of Failure / Fearful of Disappearing

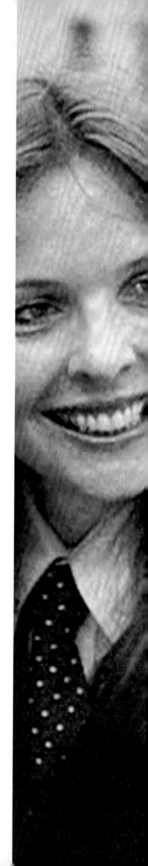

- It's pretty hard to commit to another person if you don't know who you are or what you want.
- That "becoming one" aspect of marriage or commitment can sure seem like losing your own self — so work together to figure out how not to do that.
- Rather than looking at it as 1+1 = 1, think 1+1 = endless possibilities.

QUOTABLE

Woody Allen: It's different because you keep your own apartment. Because you know, it's there. We don't have to go to it, we don't have to deal with it, but it's like a free-floating life raft that we know we're not married.

THE STORY

What a confused, insecure fellow Woody Allen plays in this movie. First he's concerned no woman would want him and then he's concerned Diane Keaton might want him, so he throws up barriers against her. Poor thing: As much as he wants to be accepted he fears being absorbed. But hey, if you don't commit and you don't get married then you won't have to face the pain of breaking up or divorce, right? There are plenty of funny lines and situations in this classic romantic comedy whose main message seems to be that we are often our own worst enemies when it comes to finding and keeping love. A possible solution? Have brave hearts and dare to try for joy. Like the old saying goes: "Nothing ventured, nothing gained."

RUNAWAY BRIDE

JULIA ROBERTS:
... you knew the real me.

RICHARD GERE:
Yes, I did.

RELEASE DATE
1999

BRIEF DESCRIPTION
Julia Roberts keeps leaving guys at the altar and Richard Gere arrives to write a story about that; along the way they discover what motivates them... including both attraction and fear of commitment.

CAST
Richard Gere (Ike Graham), Julia Roberts (Maggie Carpenter)

LOVER TYPES
Skittish / Confused / Observant / Patient / High-Spirited

- Trying to be who you think other people want you to be is ultimately fruitless.
- The institution of marriage actually can swallow people up — but it doesn't have to if you go in with eyes open and mind working in addition to heart fluttering.
- Once you know who you really are and what you really want, you likely won't lose yourself in a relationship.

QUOTABLE

Julia Roberts: When I was walking down the aisle, I was walking toward somebody who didn't have any idea who I really was. And it was only half the other person's fault, because I had done everything to convince him that I was exactly what he wanted. So it was good that I didn't go through with it because it would have been a lie. But you did — you knew the real me.
Richard Gere: Yes, I did.
Julia Roberts: I didn't. And you being the one at the end of the aisle didn't just fix that.

THE STORY

Though many times engaged and marching up that aisle, Julia Roberts just can't quite make it all the way to the altar. Richard Gere arrives to write an article about this Runaway Bride. Because marriage is at base a legalized business institution for ensuring the care of children, the orderly passing down of property, and in too many situations the treatment of females as property, it's no wonder there's a deep-seated often unconscious fear about it for many women. For Julia to go from being her free self to being "wife" and "mother" does look scary. Richard's investigation helps her realize more about herself than she has hitherto explored or admitted and in the course of his research on her they begin to fall for each other. Julia also leaves him at the altar though, because she still hasn't figured out who she really is. Once she does that and is secure enough to know she will not become lost in an institution, it's she who proposes to Richard. And this time there actually is a wedding.

TRAIN-WRECK

AMY SCHUMER:
*Why do I feel like...
so scared?*

RELEASE DATE
2015

BRIEF DESCRIPTION
Amy Schumer is the child of divorced parents who has decided never to go down that road... until she meets good guy Bill Hader and starts falling for him. Fearful of how it might end, they're both afraid to take the next steps, but thank goodness for wise friends like LeBron James.

CAST
Amy Schumer (Amy), Bill Hader (Aaron), LeBron James (himself)

LOVER TYPES
Disillusioned / Commitment Phobic / Kinda Crazy / The Nice One / Afraid to Trust / Sees the Best in the Other

- Don't let your parents' mistakes rule your love life.
- It can be rough going to get through the other person's defense shields but if you're drawn strongly to them, do go for it.
- A close friend may have more insight and good advice about your relationship than you can because you're so immersed in the situation. Listen to them.

QUOTABLE

Amy Schumer: I like him so much. Why do I feel like... so scared?

THE STORY

Amy Schumer's parents divorced when she was a very young girl and the watchword from her dad was "Monogamy isn't realistic." She's living her love map with that as her home truth, despite seeing her sister in a happy marriage. Amy's watchword is "Love 'em and leave 'em." Or in her case, have sex with 'em and leave 'em. Oh, and be just as wild and crazy all the time as you possibly can and don't worry about self-respect or other people's feelings, either. Then, on a writing assignment for a men's magazine, she meets and starts falling for sports doctor Bill Hader, a really nice guy who really likes her. As the feeling becomes mutual and more intense, Amy senses herself sliding down that slippery slope and is driving herself and others crazy with her painfully amusing dance of approach, retreat: two steps forward, five steps back, try again — no don't! Bill has his own problems opening up and trusting this unpredictable woman. A bonus is watching Bill with his good friend LeBron James (yes, the real-live basketball champion), who helps both him and Amy realize what's most important to them and what they should do about it — typically in rather funny fashion. Stepping out from the shadow of our parents' mistakes can be really, really freeing. It works here.

BREAK-FAST AT TIFFANY'S

GEORGE PEPPARD:

You know what's wrong with you, Miss Whoever-you-are? You're chicken, you've got no guts.

RELEASE DATE
1961

BRIEF DESCRIPTION

Audrey Hepburn escaped a small-town marriage and is determined to be fancy-free in New York City but finds herself falling for not-yet-successful writer George Peppard, who's also there to make his way to independence. Can their determination to stay uncommitted and available to whatever withstand the growing attraction between them?

CAST

Audrey Hepburn (Holly Golightly), George Peppard (Paul Varjak)

A Runaway from Marriage / Moody / Self-Destructive / Passionate / Determined / Insecure / Yearning Yet Fearful

LOVE LESSONS

- We are prisoners of our own desires and fears.
- Seeing ourselves in someone else and accepting them can lead to self-acceptance.
- If what you've decided is making you miserable, reconsider your decision.

QUOTABLE

George Peppard: You know what's wrong with you, Miss Whoever-you-are? You're chicken, you've got no guts. You're afraid to stick out your chin and say, "Okay, life's a fact, people do fall in love, people do belong to each other, because that's the only chance anybody's got for real happiness." You call yourself a free spirit, a wild thing, and you're terrified somebody's gonna stick you in a cage. Well, baby, you're already in that cage. You built it yourself. And it's not bounded in the west by Tulip, Texas, or in the east by Somali-land. It's wherever you go. Because no matter where you run, you just end up running into yourself.

THE STORY

In this multi-award-winning movie, Audrey Hepburn is a flighty sophisticated girl who ran away to New York City from a loveless marriage in small-town Texas and is now intent on using her charms to surround herself with money and fine things. Handsome George Peppard is a mostly unsuccessful writer and somewhat of a kept man. These two mirror each other and their initial friendship starts to grow into something more romantic. But both have agendas for success that do not include commitments... Audrey won't even name her cat. Wins and setbacks affect them both and it's up and down until a final confrontation that looks at first like an angry good-bye but resolves in a passionate, accepting kiss. Sometimes the mirror of love can show us who we really are and then turn into a window to show us what we can become.

CHAPTER 15

Get Me to the Church on Time... Or Not

MY BEST FRIEND'S WEDDING

JULIA ROBERTS:
I have to be ruthless.

RELEASE DATE
1997

BRIEF DESCRIPTION

Julia Roberts tries to break up her best friend Dermot Mulroney's wedding because she wants him for herself... or so she thinks. When her attempts backfire she learns important things about herself, and about real love.

CAST

Julia Roberts (Julianne Potter), Dermot Mulroney (Michael O'Neal), Rupert Everett (George Downes), Cameron Diaz (Kimberly Wallace)

LOVER TYPES

Self-Centered / Possessive / Win-at-All-Costs / Platonic / Sure / Gay / Innocent

- You can't make someone love you if that possibility isn't already in them. Really, you can't.
- Don't destroy other people's happiness for your own selfish reasons.
- Don't mistake the love between friends for romance, but never discount the joy of wonderful friendships.

QUOTABLE

Julia Roberts: This is my whole life's happiness. I have to be ruthless.

THE STORY

Sometimes we confuse like with love and vice versa. When her best friend gets engaged, Julia Roberts sets out to sabotage his wedding. After all, she and Dermot Mulroney had promised to marry each other years ago, then drifted apart. And after all, sometimes we just don't want someone until we can't have them anymore. Antics ensue, true love is endangered, and confusions arise. Her best friend, Rupert Everett, offers sage advice, and Julia actually comes to realize that bride-to-be Cameron Diaz is perfect for Dermot. Soul-searching reveals hidden truths, and eventually true friendship prevails over jealousy and insecurity. It's a really good idea to figure out why you're desperate to "have" someone before you do something that may destroy the happiness of many people... and often yourself included.

IN & OUT

KEVIN KLINE:

I just came out! At my wedding!

RELEASE DATE

1997

BRIEF DESCRIPTION

High school teacher Kevin Kline doesn't realize he's gay but how he finds out and admits it makes for a fun, sweet story... except for his fiancée, Joan Cusack, who's left at the altar. Will she find comfort elsewhere? Will family, friends, and the town accept him? And how about that dynamite kiss with Tom Selleck?

CAST

Kevin Kline (Howard Brackett), Tom Selleck (Peter Malloy), Joan Cusack (Emily Montgomery)

Shy / Clueless / Kind / People Pleaser / Insecure / Confused / Worldly / Accepting / Loyal

- Do some serious self-exploration before you start doing serious things like marriage.
- If something about the situation doesn't seem quite right, it just might not be, so open your eyes to who you both really are.
- Self-acceptance can positively affect how others see and treat you.

Kevin Kline: I just came out! At my wedding!

They're just not that into you. Why? Well... maybe he/she/they are gay/lesbian/bi... whatever. Small-town high school teachers Kevin Kline and Joan Cusack have dated for years but never, well, you know. She thinks it's just because he's shy. He thinks so too — until he's outed by a former student turned movie star. Kevin begins to discover who he really is as his family, students, the administration, and the whole town are thrown into a turmoil. He really spins out when reporter Tom Selleck kisses him, for real. After that there's no denying it — he is gay and he announces it at the altar. So there goes that wedding, sending Joan out on a well-deserved but quite funny pity party. Then, despite the persecution from a few close-minded people, many of Kevin's family, friends, and students stand up to support him, no matter who or how he is. Authenticity wins the day with loyalty and a sense of humor. The lesson here? Know your intended, but more important — know yourself.

THE PRINCESS BRIDE

ROBIN WRIGHT:
I will never doubt again.

CARY ELWES:
*There will never
be a need.*

RELEASE DATE
1987

BRIEF DESCRIPTION

In this perennial favorite, young lovers Cary Elwes and Robin Wright are separated; then he's presumed dead and she's being forced to marry the evil prince. But the fates intervene in really fun ways with pirates, a giant, sword fights, talkative villains, political intrigue, cliff-hangers, and maybe, possibly, lovers reunited. Something for everyone!

CAST

Robin Wright (Buttercup), Cary Elwes (Westley), Mandy Patinkin (Inigo Montoya), Chris Sarandon (Prince Humperdinck)

LOVER TYPES

Devoted / Loyal / Valiant / Innocent /
Grieving / Honorable / Power-Hungry /
Manipulative

LOVE LESSONS

- If you're in too big of a hurry to
  get to the altar you just might miss
  something important.
- That special love between two people
  can inspire other people to courage
  and honor.
- If it's real, it lasts forever.

QUOTABLE

Cary Elwes: I told you I would always come
for you. Why didn't you wait for me?
Robin Wright: Well... you were dead.
Cary Elwes: Death cannot stop true love. All
it can do is delay it for a while.
Robin Wright: I will never doubt again.
Cary Elwes: There will never be a need.

THE STORY

In this romantic, adventurous, fighting,
sports, dueling, clever story, young
farmhand Cary Elwes and beautiful farmer's
daughter Robin Wright are in love. He
leaves to seek his fortune, promising to
return and marry her, but Robin hears he's
been taken by pirates and is presumed
dead. Right before her wedding to a
smarmy prince, Robin is kidnapped by a
giant, a swordsman, and a talkative villain.
They're pursued by a man in black who
challenges and bests all three kidnappers,
then reveals himself as Robin's true love,

Cary. Turns out the prince set up the kidnapping to start a war. When captured by the prince, Robin promises to marry him in return for Cary's freedom but her sacrifice is for naught as Cary is promptly tortured to (near) death. Rescued by the former kidnappers, he's sort of brought back to life, and they're off to try to rescue Robin. Many brave, outlandish, noble, comedic events follow, including sword fights, ghosts (?), reunions, escape attempts, and yes... magical true-love kisses. There are many quotable lines from "As you wish," to "You keep using that word. I do not think it means what you think it means," to the oft-repeated "My name is Inigo Montoya. You killed my father. Prepare to die."

FOUR WED-DINGS AND A FUNERAL

HUGH GRANT:

Why am I always at weddings and never actually getting married....

RELEASE DATE

1994

BRIEF DESCRIPTION

For a person who spends so much time at weddings you'd think at least once Hugh Grant would have been the groom. But he still hasn't. Why? He wonders that himself and begins a journey of increasing self-awareness. Will it lead him to the altar? Will it be with the right woman?

CAST

Hugh Grant (Charles), Andie MacDowell (Carrie), John Hannah (Matthew), Kristin Scott Thomas (Fiona)

LOVER TYPES

Hesitant / Always the Bachelor / Clueless / Confident / Surprised by Passion

- Marriage is different for everybody. Don't rule out the possibility of it working for you just because you haven't seen what you think you want in other people's marriages.
- Before you blame your single state on other people, take a good look at yourself, your attitudes, and your actions. Maybe it's you who has put up barriers to a loving relationship.
- Ideally marriage is about what's between those two people, not anybody else's expectations. Don't settle for less than joyful, passionate love — whether or not it's in a marriage.

QUOTABLE

Hugh Grant: Why am I always at weddings and never actually getting married, Matt?

John Hannah: It's probably 'cause you're a bit scruffy. Or it could also be 'cause you haven't met the right girl.

Hugh Grant: Ah, but you see, is that it? Maybe I have met the right girls. Maybe I meet the right girls all the time. Maybe it's me.

THE STORY

It seems Hugh Grant does nothing but attend other people's weddings (to which he's always late), but he's never in a solid relationship himself and shies away from his own and others' emotions. Then Andie MacDowell enters their circle of friends and he begins to see the possibility of love in a new way. Though they've had a fling, she marries someone else and old friend Kristin Scott Thomas declares her so far unrequited love for Hugh. His emotional walls are weakened at the funeral of a dear friend being eulogized by his longtime companion. Seeming now to awaken to love, Hugh will marry Kristin. Except once actually at the altar as a bridegroom he realizes and admits to all that he's really in love with Andie, and now that she's available again... He is brave enough to do something others might think is stupid or wrong. He calls off his own wedding and wins true love as well as the chance to become a different, more mature person, even if he and Andie never actually marry. The lesson here: It's about love itself, not the institutions that surround it or other people's expectations about it or us.

SECTION FOUR

"I must go where desire is burning."

RICHARD WAGNER, *composer/librettist of operas*
Siegfried, The Valkyrie, Parsifal, *and many more*

CHAPTER 16

Sex Changes Everything

JERRY MAGUIRE

TOM CRUISE:

You know this is going to change everything.

RELEASE DATE

1996

BRIEF DESCRIPTION

When outgoing sports agent Tom Cruise goes all idealistic and is unceremoniously tossed from his company, his shy coworker Renée Zellweger, who idolizes him, follows and offers to help build his new freelance agency. Along the way, romance starts to bloom.

CAST

Tom Cruise (Jerry Maguire'), Renée Zellweger (Dorothy Boyd), Cuba Gooding Jr. (Rod Tidwell)

LOVER TYPES

Type A Ambitious / Shy Admirer / The Realistic One / Insecure / "Not My Type"

- Look before you leap into a relationship.
- Ideals are hard to live up to, but worth it in the end.
- Be willing to change yourself and be willing for others to change too.

QUOTABLE

Tom Cruise: You know this is going to change everything.
Renée Zellweger: Promise?

THE STORY

There's a really good reason there are rules against dating coworkers: Sex changes everything. Sports agent Tom Cruise goes all idealistic and is unceremoniously tossed from his company. Impressed by his stand, coworker Renée Zellweger follows and offers to help build his new freelance agency. She idolizes him; he's just trying to survive in a cutthroat business. But he connects awfully well with her adorable son and begins to see Renée's worth not only as a professional but also as a person. Kinda. Sorta. She's fallen for him and he's, well, vulnerable. And yet there's that undeniable if unacknowledged attraction. Yep, inevitably, they drift toward the bedroom. Both know that because their lives are so intertwined, once they cross that sex border it's going to affect everything. Yet they're brave enough to choose possible joy over rather dry propriety. They pay a price and it isn't all easygoing, but ultimately what sex changed for them was it removed the wall that kept them from the true partnership that had drawn them together in the first place. Not a bad idea to do a bit of looking forward before taking that leap.

FRIENDS WITH BENEFITS

MILA KUNIS:

You swear you don't want anything more from me than sex?

RELEASE DATE
2011

BRIEF DESCRIPTION

Justin Timberlake and Mila Kunis are in a professional relationship, then they're roommates, then friends. And then there's some sport sex (mostly involving tennis metaphors) that threatens/promises to turn into something else entirely.

CAST

Justin Timberlake (Dylan), Mila Kunis (Jamie)

LOVER TYPES

Casual / Friendly / Affectionate / Guarded / Hopeful

- Amazing sex is like superglue and nitroglycerin — be very careful with it.
- When you open yourself up to someone, you open yourself up to someone.
- Friendship can provide a safe foundation when the sexual sparks start to fly.

QUOTABLE

Mila Kunis: You swear you don't want anything more from me than sex?

THE STORY

Headhunter Mila Kunis has recruited artist Justin Timberlake from LA to New York. The business aspect quickly grows into friendship and before long, to friends who can share a bit of sport sex because it's just "like a game of tennis," right? Both of them have relationship issues so this situation seems ideal. At first. But then... sure enough, the attraction and affection of people who actually do like each other plus the superglue of good sex starts to set in and the instinctual desire for deeper connection comes to the surface. What to do? There's a saying in metaphysics that "when you have sex with someone you download their karma." That'll give most of us pause. Regardless of the karma bit, it's pretty obvious that in this film and in many real-life situations having sex with someone radically changes the dynamic of a relationship for one or both people. It's supposed to! So just keep that in mind when you're thinking of stepping across that border and be sure you're okay to deal with the possibility of your entire world changing.

MOON-STRUCK

NICOLAS CAGE:
The only thing that's here is you — and me.

RELEASE DATE
1987

BRIEF DESCRIPTION
Both Cher and her fiancé's brother, Nicolas Cage, are surprised and overwhelmed by their mutual sexual attraction. Now how are they going to deal with all the changes it's going to make in all the lives around them?

CAST
Cher (Loretta Castorini), Nicolas Cage (Ronny Cammareri)

LOVER TYPES
Loner / Rebellious / Reluctant / Irresistible / Romantic / Possessed by Passion

- Passion sometimes strikes with no warning, no basis, no rhyme, and no reason.
- The most passionate loves are those we are powerless to resist.
- If you're lucky and brave enough to try, other parts of your life may become infused with the same high energy of the sexual attraction.

QUOTABLE

Nicolas Cage: Everything seems like nothing to me now, 'cause I want you in my bed. I don't care if I burn in hell. I don't care if you burn in hell. The past and the future is a joke to me now. I see that they're nothing. I see they ain't here. The only thing that's here is you — and me.

THE STORY

Cher is engaged to a man she likes but does not love. When he leaves town to visit distant family, he asks her to convince his estranged brother, Nicolas Cage, to come to the wedding. Their first meeting is tempestuous. Very tempestuous. She cooks for him, they argue, and then fall into bed together. Yep, sex is changing things here all right. As opposed to the slow build in other stories, this is instant, undeniable, earth-shattering, life-changing surrender to a very strong mutual attraction, and the rest of the movie is about what happens after that passionate turning point. Sex changes your life the way turning a kaleidoscope changes all the pieces and positions and creates new patterns. Things will never be the same — but that can be a very good and joyful thing.

WHEN HARRY MET SALLY...

BILLY CRYSTAL:

No man can be friends with a woman whom he finds attractive.

RELEASE DATE
1989

BRIEF DESCRIPTION

Meg Ryan and Billy Crystal are longtime friends with diametrically opposed views on love, romance, and sex. And then the possibility of sex between the two of them threatens/promises to change everything.

CAST

Meg Ryan (Sally Albright), Billy Crystal (Harry Burns)

LOVER TYPES

Cocky / Love 'Em and Leave 'Em / Confirmed Romantic / Unfulfilled / Still Searching / Reluctant

- Yes, men and women can be good friends without sex.
- Yes, men and women can still be good friends even with sex.
- When you get past the basic biological drives into the higher levels of friendship, respect, and caring — adding good sex can improve all other parts of a relationship.

Billy Crystal: No man can be friends with a woman whom he finds attractive. He always wants to have sex with her.

In this iconic and rather ironic rom-com Billy Crystal tries to enlighten Meg Ryan about a man's view of women. Well, his view anyway. She's skeptical and a firm romantic so there'll be nothing between them. Over the years they meet up and dance around the friends/lovers issue, giving each other insights into both sides. Can there really be such a thing as pure friendship between a man and a woman? Once they actually are friends, does that mean he doesn't find her attractive anymore? With snappy dialogue and some unforgettable scenes this film explores that age-old question. For years Meg and Billy manage to keep sex out of the picture and do become better and better friends. Then she suffers a breakup and they have comfort sex, then split for a while because, sure enough, sex did change things. Happily though, when they do reunite both have shifted perspective and they come together romantically on a solid foundation of a long-term friendship. So after all those years of no sex and then having sex? Seems like it brought into sharper focus the value they found in each other and added joy to the complex equation of their relationship.

CHAPTER 17

Torn Between Two Lovers?

WHILE YOU WERE SLEEPING

SANDRA BULLOCK:
It's just... I never met anyone I could laugh with.

RELEASE DATE
1995

BRIEF DESCRIPTION
Sandra Bullock idealizes Peter Gallagher and when she finally gets to pose as his fiancée (he's in a coma), she then meets his down-to-earth brother, Bill Pullman. Before long her emotions are torn between the two of them. What's an idealistic but still yearning girl to do?

CAST
Bill Pullman (Jack), Sandra Bullock (Lucy), Peter Gallagher (Peter)

LOVER TYPES
Dreamer / Unrealistic / Idealist / Realist / Unsure of Self-Worth / Suspicious

- Ideals can be valuable to help define and keep you on track toward what you want; but if you ultimately want a real love, it helps to be realistic.
- It's hard to be in real love with someone you've placed on a pedestal. Usually all you get to kiss is their feet.
- When torn between two lovers, you need to figure out which one is really closest to your heart and not just who you — and maybe others, too — think you should be with.

QUOTABLE

Sandra Bullock: It's just... I never met anyone I could laugh with. You know?

THE STORY

Lonely singleton Sandra Bullock has been mooning over the "perfect man" Peter Gallagher, whom she sees every day as he passes her tollbooth. She saves him from being hit by a train and lets the misunderstanding ride that she is the heretofore unmet fiancée of this man in a coma. Now she falls for his eccentric family and relishes being welcomed into their world, even if it's under false pretenses. Then she meets his very awake brother, Bill Pullman, who's suspicious of this strange woman in his family's midst. But they connect so well and little by little her affections begin to shift from the dream man in a coma to the real man very much present. Peter wakes up with amnesia and still, Sandra lets the lie ride, heading toward marriage, afraid to tell the truth. Bill pulls away, hurt and still suspicious. Sandra finally comes clean at her wedding to Peter, daring to admit the truth about these two loves, both to herself and to the others. Peter was a dream she once had but now she's very much in love with Bill. It works. Often we fall in love with our idea of the other person and since few people can fulfill all of our needs (especially if they're in a coma) we sometimes keep looking for those missing bits in someone else, just trying to find perfection.

SABRINA

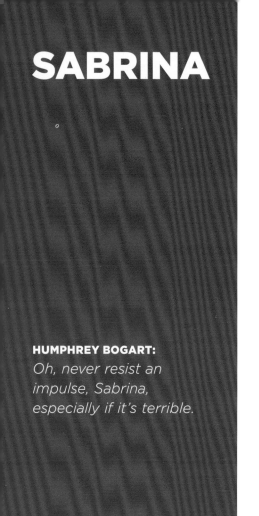

HUMPHREY BOGART:

Oh, never resist an impulse, Sabrina, especially if it's terrible.

RELEASE DATE

1954

BRIEF DESCRIPTION

Audrey Hepburn has always been infatuated with the younger playboy brother of the family her father chauffeurs for; then stodgy older brother Humphrey Bogart is sent to woo her away from an unsuitable marriage. The wooing works awfully well as Audrey becomes torn between her feelings for the two brothers: one an idealistic infatuation and the other a more mature respect and admiration.

CAST

Humphrey Bogart (Linus Larrabee), Audrey Hepburn (Sabrina Fairchild)

Idealistic / Infatuated / Stuffy and
Stodgy / Insecure / Confident /
Exuberant / Reluctant / In Love with
Someone Else

LOVE LESSONS

- A checklist of plus and minus for each
  person can help you compare and see
  more clearly.
- Given the right opportunity, many
  seemingly stodgy or reserved people
  will reveal depths of passion, and it'll
  mean all the more because it's rare
  for them.
- Pay more attention to your actual
  current feelings than to the
  remembrance of your former feelings.
  You change. Others change. Feelings
  change. Act on the now, not the past.

QUOTABLE

Humphrey Bogart: Why are you looking at
me that way?
Audrey Hepburn: All night long I've had
the most terrible impulse to do something.
Humphrey Bogart: Oh, never resist an
impulse, Sabrina, especially if it's terrible.

THE STORY

All her life Audrey Hepburn, the chauffeur's
daughter, has been madly in love with
the ne'er-do-well younger son of the
wealthy family on whose estate she and
her widowed father live. When he blithely
rejects her she even tries suicide but that
fails and she goes off to Paris. Once she

returns, transformed from heartbroken tomboy into a sophisticated young woman, her sights are still set on the younger brother. Then, straitlaced older brother Humphrey Bogart starts paying attention to her. She doesn't know his parents have ordered him to keep her away from his brother. Audrey's natural high spirits enliven stodgy Humphrey even as he tries to deny his growing attractions for this unsuitable much-younger woman. Meanwhile, she finds herself growing more attracted to his calm, respectful strength of character. But she's still in love with the younger brother, too. Isn't she? What's a girl to do? How can she choose between these two lovers? Audrey dares to move on from a childhood dream to a grown-up reality but it all only sorts out at the last minute in this classic romantic comedy. Particularly if one of the people we're infatuated with doesn't seem to love us back, it's probably time to step back and take a look at the reality of things. And if we're lucky, our love can be twice as joyful with that other quite real person.

BRIDGET JONES'S DIARY

COLIN FIRTH:

*I like you, very much.
Just as you are.*

RELEASE DATE

2001

BRIEF DESCRIPTION

Renée Zellweger is torn between sexy bad boy Hugh Grant and handsome, steadfast Colin Firth. One feeds her wild side, the other pulls her toward her better self. Who'll win this internal and external contest?

CAST

Renée Zellweger (Bridget Jones), Colin Firth (Mark Darcy), Hugh Grant (Daniel Cleaver)

LOVER TYPES

Neurotic / Fun-Loving / Insecure / Self-Critical / Cad / Narcissist / Sedate / Perceptive / Supportive

- Sure, the dark side is attractive and fun to explore, up to a point; but it's not a place to stay and the sooner we realize that the better off we'll be.
- Make a list of each person's character traits and rate them "appealing" or "appalling."
- Between the person who expects you to fulfill their desires and the one who wants to help you fulfill your own desires — which do you really think is best for you?

QUOTABLE

Colin Firth: I don't think you're an idiot at all. I mean, there are elements of the ridiculous about you.... You really are an appallingly bad public speaker. And, um, you tend to let whatever's in your head come out of your mouth without much consideration of the consequences.... But the thing is, um, what I'm trying to say, very inarticulately, is that, um, in fact, perhaps despite appearances, I like you, very much. Just as you are.

THE STORY

Poor Renée Zellweger is a mess of unmet expectations. She goes on a campaign of self-improvement, irreverently chronicled in her diary. Lose weight, cut back on drinking and smoking, be neater and cleaner, be less eccentric, and find a good man who really is good — and dashingly handsome as well. Not too much to ask for, right? Unless you're a scatterbrained chatterbox unsure of your own worth and unclear on your own identity and... well, that's her. Renée is lucky, though, that two very different men find her attractive — her boss, Hugh Grant, a bounder and a cad but very sexy, and Colin Firth, a buttoned-down attorney and longtime family friend, handsome and steadfast. The poor girl is torn between the two and doesn't know what to do... for quite an entertaining while. Then the fact that Colin actually likes her just as she is gives her the perspective and the strength to accept herself too, and simultaneously make some positive changes — like letting go of bad boy Hugh and going for the stronger, surer love. It's said we often find attractive in others what we ourselves do not embody. Taking a look at what it is we find appealing in each of the two lovers can give insight into what might actually be in our own best interest.

MISS PETTIGREW LIVES FOR A DAY

FRANCES MCDORMAND:

I am not an expert on love, I am an expert on the lack of love....

RELEASE DATE

2008

BRIEF DESCRIPTION

Actress-singer Amy Adams lives in a glamorous swirl of juggling three very different men, all offering attractive things and situations. Fortunately, her social secretary is the more experienced Frances McDormand, whose advice about what's really important in love might possibly help Amy decide.

CAST

Amy Adams (Delysia Lafosse), Frances McDormand (Guinevere Pettigrew), Mark Strong (Nick), Ciarán Hinds (Joe)

Flighty / Indecisive / Ambitious / Serious / Wounded / Dangerous / Manipulative / Narcissistic / Sincere / Forgiving / Hesitant / Loyal

- Love should not be a commodity traded in for furs, jewels, or jobs.
- The sooner you figure out what a lover really wants from you and whether or not you're willing to give that, the sooner you'll be able to decide whom to be with.
- Don't let confusion over choices take you off track from your ultimate goal: true, loyal, passionate love for and between you and a beloved.

Frances McDormand: You people, with your green drinks and your parties and your subterfuges! You're all playing at love. One minute her, the next minute someone else, flit, flit, flit! Well, I'm not playing. Love is not a game.... I am not an expert on love, I am an expert on the lack of love, Delysia, and that is a fate from which I wish most fervently to save you.

Only two lovers? How mundane. Actress and singer Amy Adams is juggling three men: a spoiled young producer staging a show she hopes to star in by paying it forward with her considerable "charms"; the gangsterish and possessive owner of

the classy nightclub where she sings
(who also provides her with a very nice
apartment, furs, and jewels); and her loyal
longtime friend and former boyfriend, a
poor piano player who wants to marry
her and take her back to America where
they can both pursue their artistic careers
in freedom. Ambition, survival, love,
security, fame, fortune, integrity — it's all
on the table and all in conflict. Once she
chooses one man she'll lose the other two
and all that they offer. What is she willing
to give up? What does she really want?
Fortunately for Amy she has an objective
advisor in her social secretary, Frances
McDormand (Miss Pettigrew), an older
woman whose own personal losses have
made her wise about love. Sometimes
the most valuable perspective on our
situation comes from someone who can
see both the bigger picture and how we
might best fit into it, with the best results.
Love can last a lifetime; those other
things do not.

CHAPTER 18

For Love or Money?

PRETTY WOMAN

RICHARD GERE:
You and I are such similar creatures, Vivian.

RELEASE DATE
1990

BRIEF DESCRIPTION
Businessman Richard Gere hires prostitute Julia Roberts as an escort during his corporate deal-making and all is quite professional, until they start to get to know each other....

CAST
Julia Roberts (Vivian Ward), Richard Gere (Edward Lewis)

LOVER TYPES
User / Hard-Nosed Professional / Working Girl / Pride Battling Insecurity / Surface Friendly — Inwardly Unavailable / Closed Off from Self / Exuberant

- "It's only business" only works if you keep it only business.
- Personal revelations, fun and laughter, and sharing insights tend to shift the nature of a relationship, often bringing out the better side of both parties.
- People have certain boundaries (like not kissing on the mouth in Julia's case) and when those barriers start to fall you know everything's about to change.

QUOTABLE

Richard Gere: You and I are such similar creatures, Vivian. We both screw people for money.

THE STORY

Julia Roberts is a sex worker picked up by wealthy corporate raider Richard Gere, who quickly seeing her beauty and wit, hires her to be his escort while he's in town doing business deals. He funds her Beverly Hills shopping spree so she can dress appropriately and she surely does play the part well at dinners, the opera, and in meetings. In conversations and sexual encounters over the week, they get to know each other better and the business arrangement starts to become personal as she helps bring out a better part of himself. When she knows they're really in love, Julia allows kissing on the mouth and this time instead of just having sex, they really make love. In the original script Richard left town without her and Julia went back to the streets; but in this exceptionally popular rom-com, both of them end up with both love and money. Once again, it's about letting go of stereotypes and expectations and seeing beyond the surface, deeper into the other person's heart.

THAT TOUCH OF MINK

RELEASE DATE

1962

BRIEF DESCRIPTION

Playboy Cary Grant showers naïve Doris Day with clothes, gifts, and a trip to the Caribbean, expecting in return her charms and favors. It's a seesaw of nervous encounters, approaches-retreats, and growing attraction. Now if only they can actually really get together. Like, really, romantically.

CAST

Cary Grant (Philip Shayne), Doris Day (Cathy Timberlake), Audrey Meadows (Connie Emerson)

LOVER TYPES

Naïve / Well-Meaning Manipulator / Playboy / Virgin on the Verge / Willing to Explore / Opening to Respect for Others

AUDREY MEADOWS:
What can you expect from a man like that?

DORIS DAY:
Respect.

- Be willing to explore beyond what society tells you are the boundaries of proper behavior.
- Hold on to your deepest sense of integrity in the face of attractive temptations — at least until you can determine the value of those temptations.
- For people of differing value systems, stepping for a while into each other's mindset can often bring both to that place of willing compromise where romance resides.

QUOTABLE

Audrey Meadows: Cathy. A man picks you up off the street, drags you up to his office, tricks you into taking your clothes off, and then propositions you. What can you expect from a man like that?
Doris Day: Respect.
Audrey Meadows: Respect. On that note of logic, I'll go to work.

THE STORY

Doris Day is a naïve, currently unemployed young woman being pursued by wealthy businessman Cary Grant, who is used to buying everything from loyalty in his employees to female companionship. Her friend Audrey Meadows tries to warn her that he's only after one thing but Doris is both quite attracted to him and thinks maybe it's time she becomes a more modern woman. She accepts the glamorous clothes and a trip to the Caribbean but when the time comes she's so nervous about having sex that she breaks out in a rash. The next time they try she gets falling-down drunk. Cary meanwhile has become truly enamored of her and finds himself changing his mind about it all. He really comes to respect her, proposes marriage, and on their wedding night, this time he breaks out in a rash. Being willing to test our own boundaries can help us open to new possibilities. But keeping our own integrity is what can bring self-esteem and sometimes, like in this story, true love.

BREAK-FAST AT TIFFANY'S

AUDREY HEPBURN:

Ahh... Do I detect a look of disapproval in your eye?

RELEASE DATE

1961

BRIEF DESCRIPTION

Audrey Hepburn and George Peppard are both trading sex for money when they become friends. As friendship turns to love both struggle to discover and live out their true values... but both find that really hard to do.

CAST

Audrey Hepburn (Holly Golightly), George Peppard (Paul Varjak)

LOVER TYPES

Flighty / Moody / Self-Destructive / Fearful of Intimacy / Awakening to Love / Social Climber / Frustrated Artiste / Sex-for-Money

- Money can buy a lot of things, but love and happiness are not on that list.
- Sex, money, and love are not currencies of equal value and should not be mistaken as such.
- Though sure, we all need to survive, love takes us above and beyond the material world.

QUOTABLE

Audrey Hepburn: Ahh... Do I detect a look of disapproval in your eye? Tough beans, buddy, 'cause that's the way it's gonna be.

THE STORY

George Peppard and Audrey Hepburn are both selling themselves. He's a struggling writer kept by a wealthy older woman and she is, well, a high-class call girl. When he moves into her apartment building they become friends and soon figure out each other's career paths and the reasons for it. He's trying to support himself so he can keep writing; she wants to take in her brother once he's out of the Army. As the friendship grows, so does their attraction for each other. Audrey becomes the mistress of a wealthy man but George breaks off his money-for-sex arrangement. He declares his love for Audrey but she's afraid of getting close and rebuffs his proposal. He calls her on that and stalks away. In tears and remorse, she goes after him and they embrace. Their kisses with others used to be for money; now kissing each other... that's just about love. Sure, people need money. But time and again we see that after the basic needs are met, we need love a whole lot more than we need more money. Getting straight on what it is you really want and need can make all the difference in the world.

WORKING GIRL

RELEASE DATE
1988

BRIEF DESCRIPTION
Secretary Melanie Griffith really wants to rise in the world of finance and on the way up meets a man she really wants, too. Unbeknownst to her, Harrison Ford is her manipulative boss's estranged boyfriend and soon there's a territorial battle over both professional power and the man.

CAST
Melanie Griffith (Tess McGill), Harrison Ford (Jack Trainer), Sigourney Weaver (Katharine Parker)

MELANIE GRIFFITH:
I have a head for business and a bod for sin.

Ambitious / Daring / Unsure / Growing Confidence /
Entitled / Oblivious / Vain / Manipulative / Suave /
Surprised / Considerate / Supportive

LOVE LESSONS

- Power or Passion — must you choose between the
  two? Maybe it's not either-or but both-and.
- When you're right you have to stand up for
  yourself, regardless of what you think you may lose.
- Money, position, and power can all be positive
  things — in the right hands with the right motives.

QUOTABLE

Melanie Griffith: I have a head for business and a bod
for sin. Is there anything wrong with that?
Harrison Ford: Uh, no. No.

THE STORY

Melanie Griffith is a business whiz but is stuck as a
secretary. Her new boss, Sigourney Weaver, takes her
idea for a financial merger and is going to claim it
as her own. But when Sigourney's out with a broken
leg, Melanie takes over her fancy home, her elegant
wardrobe, her business connections, and along the
way her boyfriend, Harrison Ford — without either
of them knowing about the mutual connections.
Still unsure in this new world of high finance and
the heady romance with Harrison, Melanie is torn
between her ambitions and her emotions. When
Sigourney returns and arrogantly claims both the idea
and the man, Melanie must find courage she isn't sure
she has within her. One thing she does know, though,
is that her financial plan was a good idea. And if she
trusts her intuition and intellect in that realm, maybe
what's happening in the romance arena is also a good
idea. Can she fight for both and win?

CHAPTER 19

Those Cheatin' Hearts — What're You Gonna Do?

LOVE ACTUALLY

EMMA THOMPSON:
Mia's very pretty.

ALAN RICKMAN:
Is she?

RELEASE DATE
2003

BRIEF DESCRIPTION
Alan Rickman's secretary is out to seduce him, and his wife, Emma Thompson, figures it out. She warns him but does not make a big fuss. Will her seeming coldness drive him toward the steamy secretary? Or will the marriage vows hold?

CAST
Alan Rickman (Harry), Emma Thompson (Karen), Heike Makatsch (Mia)

LOVER TYPES
Straying / In Need of Attention / Seductress / Domestic — Not Romantic

- No matter how long you've been in a committed relationship, attention and romance are still important.
- If people don't get what they feel they need at home, they're more vulnerable when it's offered elsewhere.
- The shallow flirtation and the threat of loss can illuminate what's really important to us.

QUOTABLE

Emma Thompson: Mia's very pretty.
Alan Rickman: Is she?
Emma Thompson: You know she is, darling. Be careful there.

THE STORY

It is a well-known fact that a man in a position of power is in need of a mistress. Alan Rickman is targeted for seduction by his overtly sexy secretary, Heike Makatsch. At first he doesn't quite seem to know what to do about her advances. His very self-controlled wife, Emma Thompson, is focused on their children and seems to be, just maybe, taking him for granted. To be overtly chased must be rather an exciting change for him. But so often the other party in a partnership twigs that something's going on and, after seeing them together at the company Christmas party, she offers a wifely warning. Perhaps Emma could tell that it wouldn't turn into a full affair, perhaps she was afraid to press the issue further, perhaps she knew their love was solid. Regardless, she chooses to focus on the marriage and ignore the blip of possible cheating. Apparently, so does Alan.

THE SEVEN YEAR ITCH

MARILYN MONROE:
If I were your wife I'd be jealous of you.

RELEASE DATE
1955

BRIEF DESCRIPTION
Marilyn Monroe is a breath of fresh air for unappreciated married man Tom Ewell, who gains self-confidence from her attentions and excitement from her double entendres and sexy presence. Now, will he do anything about it?

CAST
Marilyn Monroe (The Girl), Tom Ewell (Richard Sherman)

LOVER TYPES
Bimbo / Good-Hearted / Really Does Like Men / Unappreciated / Insecure / Tempted but Timid

- If someone's feeling unappreciated, their spouse would do well to be more aware of that and do something about it before the trouble begins.
- A good flirtation (attention without intention) can do wonders for a man's self-esteem and needn't cross inappropriate barriers.
- Cheating is a choice; sometimes just admitting to yourself that you're tempted is enough to turn you away from actually doing it.

QUOTABLE

Marilyn Monroe: You think a girl goes to a party and there's some guy in a fancy striped vest strutting around giving you that I'm-so-handsome-you-can't-resist-me look. From this she's supposed to fall flat on her face. Well, she doesn't fall on her face. But there's another guy in the room, over in the corner. Maybe he's nervous and shy and perspiring a little. First, you look past him. But then you sense that he's gentle and kind and worried. That he'll be tender with you, nice and sweet. That's what's really exciting. If I were your wife I'd be jealous of you. I'd be very, very jealous.

THE STORY

Anytime people make promises there is the possibility of those promises being broken. No matter the century or the society there is a tendency of the human heart to focus on one other person and to form pair bonds, even if only for a short while. Other tendencies include the biological urge to propagate the species, the emotional urge to feel appreciated, and the more spiritual urge to find ecstatic bliss. Given the conflict these tendencies can create within the individual it's no wonder poor Tom Ewell is all in a dither when his wife and son leave the sweltering city for summer vacation and blond bombshell Marilyn Monroe moves in upstairs and pays him neighborly visits that usually include naïve double entendres and a fresh appreciation for his sweetness. His voice-over allows us to follow his troubled, funny struggles. Cheating is a choice and the humor and wisdom in this film comes from watching someone toy with temptation.

THE APART-MENT

SHIRLEY MACLAINE:

For a while there, you try kidding yourself that you're going with an unmarried man.

RELEASE DATE

1960

BRIEF DESCRIPTION

Shirley MacLaine has fallen very much in love with Fred MacMurray, then starts to suspect he's married. When she learns the shameful truth, she's devastated and searches for a way out of the pain.

CAST

Shirley MacLaine (Fran Kubelik), Jack Lemmon (C. C. Baxter), Fred MacMurray (Jeff D. Sheldrake)

LOVER TYPES

Naïve / Disillusioned / Insecure / Philanderer / Heartless / Compromising / Hopeful / Nice Guy

- Check out someone's availability before you get deeply involved.
- No matter how much you feel you love them or they claim to love you, a deceitful person can never make a good romantic love partner. A loyal, admiring, truthful person can, especially one with a sense of humor.
- Cheating: If they did it *with* you they'll like do it *to* you. Just don't go there.

QUOTABLE

Shirley MacLaine: For a while there, you try kidding yourself that you're going with an unmarried man. Then one day he keeps looking at his watch, and asks you if there's any lipstick showing, then rushes off to catch the seven-fourteen to White Plains. So you fix yourself a cup of instant coffee and you sit there by yourself, and you think, and it all begins to look so ugly.

THE STORY

Elevator girl Shirley MacLaine is very much in love with insurance executive Fred MacMurray. At first she doesn't know he's married but then the realizations start to set in and she is torn between love and shame. He says he'll leave his wife, but when she finds out she's only the latest in a long string of toss-away mistresses she tries to do away with herself, in Jack Lemmon's apartment. Jack, who really, really likes her, helps her survive and through his friendship and true admiration helps her get through it. Shirley learns through disillusionment and pain that deceit and manipulation do not make a good foundation for a romantic relationship. Honesty, affection, and respect for the other person's dignity do. So does the ability to laugh together.

THE GRASS IS GREENER

CARY GRANT:

If your wife is unfaithful, she is to be befriended.

RELEASE DATE

1960

BRIEF DESCRIPTION

English aristocrat Cary Grant's wife, Deborah Kerr, is having a fling with American Robert Mitchum while he seems to stand idly by. But Cary is a wise man who, when it comes down to it, challenges Mitchum to a duel. In this day and age?! How's that going to work out?

CAST

Cary Grant (Victor Rhyall, Earl), Deborah Kerr (Lady Hilary Rhyall), Robert Mitchum (Charles Delacro)

LOVER TYPES

Content / Complacent / Slightly Bored / Swept Away / Captured by Passion / Patient

- Into every relationship a little boredom falls, but a foundation of real love and respect can weather those dry spells.
- Sometimes actually stepping outside the domestic bonds can bring about renewed appreciation for the committed relationship.
- Give your partner their freedom, but be willing to fight for them too.

QUOTABLE

Cary Grant: If your mistress is unfaithful, she is to be discarded. If your wife is unfaithful, she is to be befriended.

THE STORY

Cary Grant and Deborah Kerr are a happily married, very civilized couple of English aristocrats holding up the tradition of opening the stately English country houses to public tours. Handsome American Robert Mitchum stumbles into the private family side and sparks fly when he and Deborah meet. She resists at first but succumbs to the lure in a discreet but decorously sizzling affair. Cary keeps a cool head and gives his beloved wife room to explore. But then he takes a stand and fights a duel for her, proving not only his undying love, but also his respect for the fact that everyone needs to make their own choices and they need room to do that. But it doesn't hurt to give a little nudge. The American respectfully leaves and the British couple reunites with enhanced respect and a revived sense of their own deep love for each other. Sometimes we need to let the other person explore on their own to discover what's really most important to them. But we should always let them know we're ready to fight for them... in a very civilized and honorable way, of course.

CHAPTER 20

Forgiveness — The Only Way to Move Forward

NOTTING HILL

JULIA ROBERTS:
I'm also just a girl, standing in front of a boy, asking him to love her.

RELEASE DATE
1999

BRIEF DESCRIPTION
Superstar Julia Roberts and shy Hugh Grant date deliriously until she mistakenly thinks he's betrayed her trust and drops him. Both hearts suffer until she returns to apologize, hoping he'll take her back.

CAST
Julia Roberts (Anna Scott), Hugh Grant (William Thacker)

LOVER TYPES
Glamorous / Wary / Yearning for Sincerity / Defensive / Shy / Humble / Sweet

LOVE LESSONS
● Public life and private life can — and probably should — be

two separate worlds. Try not to let your public persona damage your private relationships.

- Go where your heart feels joyful, regardless of what other people think.
- A humble, heartfelt apology works wonders on a wounded heart.

Hugh Grant: I live in Notting Hill. You live in Beverly Hills. Everyone in the world knows who you are. My mother has trouble remembering my name.
Julia Roberts: And don't forget... I'm also just a girl, standing in front of a boy, asking him to love her.

THE STORY

Superstar Julia Roberts has a brief but very sweet dating romance with British bookstore owner Hugh Grant, even meeting his family and friends, all rather awed he's going out with such a celebrity. Her supposed ex-boyfriend shows up and Hugh decides he can't compete with her movie-star lifestyle so he ends the budding romance. He continues life as it was, plus has some rather funny blind dates; she continues making blockbuster movies. Then Julia shows up on his doorstep to hide out from a feeding frenzy over revealing photos and a video. They delightedly make love but it's all ruined the next morning when the paparazzi descend and Julia hurriedly leaves, feeling betrayed and focusing on her reputation and not his feelings. Seasons pass and Julia is back in London filming. Visiting her on set Hugh overhears her dismissing him as "no one important." She comes to his bookstore on Notting Hill and humbles herself in a very heartfelt way, explaining she was trying to protect him from that horrid scrutiny of gossips and the press that has always been so troubling to her. At first reluctant, he does accept her apology, they do marry, and embark on a lovely life together. Sometimes we need to ask forgiveness not for what we have done, but for what we have failed to do. Why let a few words stand in the way of real love? And once those words are uttered it is incumbent upon us to respond graciously. A sincere apology can bring dignity to both people and that's a plus, regardless of the outcome of the relationship.

TWO WEEKS NOTICE

RELEASE DATE

2002

BRIEF DESCRIPTION

Developer Hugh Grant wants to demolish a community center defended by attorney Sandra Bullock. He promises to save the building if she'll be his lawyer, and more. The more is more like babysitting a spoiled child so she gives notice, further shaking up his world, which has already been shaken up by her presence. How much can one man change?

CAST

Hugh Grant (George Wade), Sandra Bullock (Lucy Kelson)

LOVER TYPES

Cavalier / Playboy / Business First / Sincere / Altruistic / Strong / Honorable

HUGH GRANT:

And even though I've said cruel things and driven her away, she's become the voice in my head.

- Don't make promises you don't seriously intend to keep.
- If you embrace an agent of change, it's bound to cause changes, so be ready.
- When you've been wrong and you sincerely apologize, the rewards may be greater than you ever imagined.

QUOTABLE

Hugh Grant: I gave my word to someone that we wouldn't knock down this building behind me. And normally, and those of you who know me or were married to me can attest to this, my word wouldn't mean very much. So why does it this time? Because this person, despite being unusually stubborn and unwilling to compromise and a very poor dresser, is... she's rather like the building she loves so much. A little rough around the edges but, when you look closely, absolutely beautiful. And the only one of her kind. And even though I've said cruel things and driven her away, she's become the voice in my head. And I can't seem to drown her out. And I don't want to drown her out.

THE STORY

Hugh Grant is a billionaire developer intent on demolishing a treasured community center. Sandra Bullock is a community activist attorney intent on saving it. He hires her because he needs a "real" lawyer on staff and then proceeds to use her to solve all sorts of problems, from big situations to wardrobe choices. Tired of being used frivolously, she gives her two weeks' notice. Tasked to train her replacement, Sandra finds herself jealous of the new girl, revealing her own more-than-business interest in Hugh. Affected by her idealism, Hugh decides to keep his promise to her to save the building. Not only do opposites often attract very strongly, they can also lead us to change something about ourselves. Hugh's public apology shows how much he has changed because of Sandra's influence. The heartfelt apology can be a bridge between ways of thinking, and between worlds.

WHAT WOMEN WANT

MEL GIBSON:
I sure wish I could read your mind.

RELEASE DATE
2000

BRIEF DESCRIPTION
When egotistical Mel Gibson can suddenly hear what women think, he's in for a shock. He's also falling for Helen Hunt but realizing she finds him despicable starts him on a path to positive change. He's got a whole lot to make up for... could she ever forgive him?

CAST
Helen Hunt (Darcy Maguire), Mel Gibson (Nick Marshall)

LOVER TYPES
Egotistical / Insensitive / Unscrupulous / Professional / Independent / Intelligent / Sincere

- A real apology is about what you did, not about what the other person feels about what you did.
- There's a real good reason so many spiritual and self-improvement systems include asking for forgiveness: It's an excellent way to let go of your former self, forgive yourself, and move on to a more positive you.
- Regardless of the other person's response, your apology will be good for you so go ahead and do it.

QUOTABLE

Mel Gibson: What if I told you that you did everything that you were hired to do — everything — but that someone was sabotaging you? Picking your brain, swiping your ideas... I took advantage of you in the worst possible way. Have you ever done that? Taken the wrong road and — No, of course you haven't. You wouldn't do that.

Helen Hunt: That's just —

Mel Gibson: Somebody like me does that. And, the problem with that was that while I was digging the hole under you, I found out all about you. And the more I found out the more you dazzled me. I mean, shook my world, changed my life, dazzled me. ... Everything about you — how smart you are, how good you are — everything just makes me want you even more.

Helen Hunt: Oh, wow. Boy.

Mel Gibson: So it looks like I'm here being all heroic trying to rescue you, but the truth is, I'm the one that needs to be rescued here. I sure wish I could read your mind.

Helen Hunt: That's it?

Mel Gibson: I don't want that to be it. I don't want that to be it at all.

Helen Hunt: Then don't let a little thing like me firing you stand in your way. I didn't know what to react to first. Hey, news flash, I took the wrong road. What kind of knight in shining armor would I be if the man I love needs rescuing and I just let him walk out my door?

Mel Gibson: My hero.

THE STORY

Mel Gibson is brash, egotistical, and insensitive to women's feelings. When his expected promotion at the ad agency goes to Helen Hunt, his thwarted ambition seeks to bring her down. Shocked in a freak encounter between a hair dryer and a bathtub, Mel can now hear what women are thinking. He listens to their hopes, dreams, insecurities, passions, and, lucky him, Helen's advertising ideas, which he steals and claims as his own. He also discovers a lot of people, men and women alike, don't like him very much. The more he learns about Helen, the more he likes her. A lot. He starts changing, becoming more sensitive and treating people with more sincerity and dignity. Along the way, he realizes he's actually falling in love with Helen. Now what to do? Another shocking accident takes away his ability to hear what females think. Sobered and encouraged by his new-found feelings, Mel courageously confesses to sabotaging Helen and asks for her forgiveness. Some apologies skirt the issue with "I'm sorry you feel that way." Mel's apology is sincere and specific, a good example to us all. And yes, she does forgive him and they do get a happy ending.

YOU'VE GOT MAIL

TOM HANKS:
You were expecting to see someone you trusted, but met the enemy instead.

RELEASE DATE
1998

BRIEF DESCRIPTION
Tom Hanks has a lot to apologize for: His bookstore chain has put Meg Ryan's indie store out of business. Then he's hit with a double whammy when he discovers she's the person he's fallen in love with online under different names. Can one apology possibly cover all that and bring the two together?

CAST
Tom Hanks (Joe Fox), Meg Ryan (Kathleen Kelly)

LOVER TYPES
Vulnerable / Shy / Ambitious / Business First / Wounded / Sincere at Heart / Apologetic

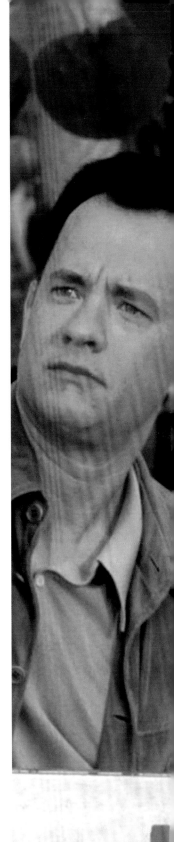

- At times our duties bring pain to others, even if we would not have it so. We can still apologize, even if part of it isn't our fault.
- To know that someone really does care about your wounded heart can be a healing thing.
- The point of apology and forgiveness is to let go of the past and move on together toward happiness.

QUOTABLE

Tom Hanks: Dear Friend, I cannot tell you what happened last night, but I beg you from the bottom of my heart to forgive me.... I feel terrible that I caused you to be in a situation that caused you additional pain.... You were expecting to see someone you trusted, but met the enemy instead. The fault is mine. Someday I will explain. Meanwhile, I'm still here. Talk to me.

THE STORY

Tom Hanks's family owns a big chain of bookstores and they're currently putting Meg Ryan's indie bookstore out of business. Simultaneously the two of them are having an online email relationship without knowing each other's identity. Tom even comes into Meg's store as just a regular customer but she soon discovers he's the guy closing down her place. She hates him for that, but still does not know this is the same person she's falling in love with online. They're in a love-hate relationship and don't even know it. Meg's bookstore goes under but her attitude toward Tom softens as she observes the positive aspects of his big store. Eventually the online personas meet, revealing it was Tom and Meg all along. Tom asks for forgiveness and it brings him closer to Meg and they become a happy couple. Sometimes we are at the mercy of forces beyond our control, but we can still take responsibility for the hurt that causes others. And for those being asked to forgive? Sometimes forgiveness is the only way to move forward.

SECTION FIVE

"Love begets love. This torment is my joy."

THEODORE ROTHKE, *award-winning poet and teacher*

CHAPTER 21

Falling in Love for the Very First Time

SOME-THING'S GOTTA GIVE

JACK NICHOLSON:

I'm sixty-three years old... and I'm in love for the first time in my life.

RELEASE DATE

2003

BRIEF DESCRIPTION

Jack Nicholson dates much younger women until he meets Diane Keaton and starts to see the value of a smart, witty, fun, warm woman his own age. Can he drop his old habits for a first chance at real love?

CAST

Jack Nicholson (Harry Sanborn), Diane Keaton (Erica Barry), Keanu Reeves (Julian Mercer)

LOVER TYPES

Egotist / Serial Seducer / Stuck in Midlife Crisis / Comfortable with Self / Successful Professional / Surprised / Resisting Change / Facing Reality / Accepting

- Change or die. It's a law of the universe. And yes, it does apply to us all.
- Growing up isn't such a bad thing and certainly doesn't mean you have to grow old.
- When you can see the other person not just as an accessory for your ego but as the individual they actually are, you're on the road to richer relationships.

QUOTABLE

Jack Nicholson: Turns out the heart attack was easy to get over. You... were something else. I finally get it. I'm sixty-three years old... and I'm in love for the first time in my life.

THE STORY

Jack Nicholson never dates anyone over thirty. Until he meets his current squeeze's mother, Diane Keaton, an attractive, successful playwright. After a heart attack Jack is confined to Diane's beach home for recuperation and they get to know each other better. To his astonishment he finds himself attracted to her wit, intelligence, beauty, and also her (gasp!) maturity. Once he's physically able to, they make love. Then he's off again and doesn't see her until she's out at a family dinner and he's with yet again a much younger woman. Diane is heartbroken but decides to turn the situation into a successful stage play and finds comfort with Jack's handsome young doctor, Keanu Reeves. Months later Jack tracks her down in Paris, where she's celebrating her birthday with Keanu. Though he adores her, the younger man sees the love between Jack and Diane and nobly steps aside. Diane finds Jack on a bridge over the River Seine and both admit their love — he for the first time in his long line of affairs.

THAT TOUCH OF MINK

CARY GRANT:
You're the type of woman who brings out the worst in a man — his conscience.

RELEASE DATE
1962

BRIEF DESCRIPTION

Playboy Cary Grant hasn't figured love into the equation of his easy, fun life until he and naïve Doris Day start falling for each other. She's old-fashioned but now wants to be more sophisticated; he's sophisticated but in a surprise to himself, actually really wants her. Where's the middle ground?

CAST

Cary Grant (Philip Shayne), Doris Day (Cathy Timberlake), Audrey Meadows (Connie Emerson)

LOVER TYPES

Naïve / Well-Meaning Manipulator / Playboy / Virgin on the Verge / Willing to Explore / Opening to Respect for Others

- Let go of what you think you know about how love should be for you.
- When you reach across an attitude gap, change goes both ways. Go with it.
- Real romantic love usually changes people for the better. If you're starting to change that way, it might just be love.

QUOTABLE

Cary Grant: You're the type of woman who brings out the worst in a man — his conscience.

THE STORY

Cary Grant is a very successful New York businessman used to lavishing attractive young women with gifts and wooing them... for a while... then moving on to the next one. Small-town transplant Doris Day is thrown into Cary's path when his limousine splashes mud on her white outfit in a bit of heavy-handed but effective symbolism. His extravagant apology gestures include an elegant wardrobe and an invitation to a weekend in the Caribbean. Still-a-virgin Doris is giddy with delight even as she wavers between succumbing to Cary's charms and holding out for marriage. Cary's debonair style starts to fray as he finds himself more and more captivated by Doris's naïveté and joy for life. Once on vacation, she breaks out in a nervous rash so nothing happens. Next time, she tries drinking to calm down but that's a disaster, too. By this time Cary's in love with her; she knows it but he won't admit it. Until she goes on a date with someone else. That does it. The playboy has fallen in love and they marry, removing the barrier to finally making love... with a comedic "maybe" at the end. When the old ways don't work for you anymore, it's time to let them go and try something new. You might even be richly rewarded.

SABRINA

RELEASE DATE
1954

BRIEF DESCRIPTION

Businessman Humphrey Bogart
is the responsible one in the
family, until exuberant Audrey
Hepburn brings light and fun
into his stodgy life. Inspired
and altered by her attitude and
their growing attraction, he
struggles to break out of his
confining mold that says love is
not for him.

CAST

Humphrey Bogart (Linus
Larrabee), Audrey Hepburn
(Sabrina Fairchild)

LOVER TYPES

Stuffy and Stodgy / Insecure /
Responsible / Confident /
Exuberant / In Love with Life

HUMPHREY BOGART:

*Paris is for lovers. Maybe
that's why I stayed only
thirty-five minutes.*

- Many older siblings take on responsibility at a young age and stay rather serious from then on. Letting go of that can open the doors for joy.
- "Falling" in love means changing positions so be prepared for some dizzying shifts in perspective and feelings.
- The right to romantic love is everybody's right regardless of age, position, background, etc.

QUOTABLE

Audrey Hepburn: Oh, but Paris isn't for changing planes, it's... it's for changing your outlook. For... for throwing open the windows and letting in... letting in *la vie en rose*.

Humphrey Bogart: Paris is for lovers. Maybe that's why I stayed only thirty-five minutes.

THE STORY

Humphrey Bogart is the conservative, dull, business-minded older brother in the wealthy family for whom Audrey's dad is the chauffeur. She's always been the cute little tomboy with a mad crush on his mischievous brother. Once back from Paris, though, she is a lovely and sophisticated young woman. Humphrey's job is to woo her himself to keep her from snagging his brother. He's new to this wooing stuff and much to his own surprise finds himself falling for her. And even more to his surprise, Audrey seems to really like him. And maybe, just maybe, more than just like. What's a self-controlled, realistic man like him to do? With some help from his younger brother, Humphrey finally decides he might as well just go with the flow and let himself fall in love. It wouldn't hurt us all to remember that "falling in love" implies a shifting of position and that real love will challenge us and change us.

TRAIN-WRECK

AMY SCHUMER:
I really wanna try with you.

RELEASE DATE
2015

BRIEF DESCRIPTION

Disillusioned about love at an early age, Amy Schumer's spent her whole life avoiding anything like romantic love. Then Bill Hader comes along and she finds herself actually really liking someone she's also attracted to. Terrifying. Until she realizes this might be how love works and maybe, just maybe...

CAST

Amy Schumer (Amy), Bill Hader (Aaron), LeBron James (himself)

LOVER TYPES

Disbeliever in Love / Commitment Phobic / The Crazy One / The Nice One / Sees the Best in the Other

- You can't love if you can't surrender.
- Be still... be still long enough to really feel something.
- Love sees what you can be, not just what you are right now.

QUOTABLE

Amy Schumer: I really wanna try with you.

THE STORY

Amy Schumer's parents divorced when she was a little girl and her dad's warning that "monogamy isn't realistic" has kept her away from romantic love and the pain it obviously entails. She never spends the whole night with someone she's just had sex with, deflects all attempts to get emotionally close, self-medicates the confusion and deep loneliness with alcohol, and is generally a pretty offensive wild-child. She's also fun, attractive, and smart. Then she meets sports doctor Bill Hader, they have sex, and he wants to see her again. Freaked out by his attentions, Amy expends a lot of energy avoiding being drawn in to someone she realizes she actually likes. It's funny but also sad. And there're some cool basketball sequences since Bill is friends with LeBron James. After her father's death, with her sister's family's encouragement, and a pep talk from LeBron, Amy is ready to admit she has fallen in love for the first time. The way she shows it is brave and funny, with a basketball flair. Much about love is surrender. Amy surrenders her resistance to real love and is on her way to passion and joy.

CHAPTER 22

Mistaken Identities

SHAKE-SPEARE IN LOVE

JOSEPH FIENNES:
Look what the dream brought us.

GWYNETH PALTROW:
It was we ourselves did that.

RELEASE DATE
1998

BRIEF DESCRIPTION
Gwyneth Paltrow pretends to be a boy in order to act onstage in Elizabethan England, while carrying on a passionate real-life affair with playwright Joseph Fiennes, who helps her maintain the disguise. Will the joys of love be worth the risk of exposure?

CAST
Gwyneth Paltrow (Viola De Lesseps), Joseph Fiennes (Will Shakespeare), Judi Dench (Queen Elizabeth)

LOVER TYPES
Artistic / Sensitive / Romantic / Idealistic / Restricted by Society / Rebellious

- We all play roles in many aspects of our lives. Who are you trying to be in your love relationships? Or not be?
- Even if you must hide your love from the world, be your true selves with each other.
- One of the joys of love is being accepted for who we really are.

QUOTABLE

Joseph Fiennes: I'm done with theatre. The playhouse is for dreamers. Look what the dream brought us.
Gwyneth Paltrow: It was we ourselves did that. And for my life to come, I would not have it otherwise.

THE STORY

In Elizabethan England females were not allowed onstage and males portrayed them, so hidden identities abounded. Stir in the betrothed beauty Gwyneth Paltrow, who's desperate to be an actress, and the blocked playwright Joseph Fiennes (as Will Shakespeare), who's desperate to write a successful play. She dresses up as a young boy and gets a role in his new play. He falls for her in her regular guise at social events, but is also drawn to the boy actor and is a bit concerned about that since he thinks he only likes women. Soon Joseph uncovers her true identity and they become secret lovers. Meanwhile, the play must go on and it does; it goes on to become *Romeo and Juliet*. This is a sigh-inducing tale of identities mistaken, revealed, reviled, and then rewarded. The only people who may ever know us are those with whom we can finally be the real us, for who does not wear many disguises and play many parts in the different aspects of our lives? But, oh, for the opportunity to do like Gwyneth and Joseph and dare to live that dream... if only for a little while.

IT HAP-PENED ONE NIGHT

CLAUDETTE COLBERT:
You've got a name, haven't you?

CLARK GABLE:
Yeah, I got a name.

RELEASE DATE
1934

BRIEF DESCRIPTION
Hiding out from the press and her controlling dad, cynical reporter Clark Gable and spoiled heiress Claudette Colbert pretend to be married and find the walls between these former strangers falling down. Might what they're pretending to be become a reality?

CAST
Clark Gable (Peter Warne), Claudette Colbert (Ellie Andrews)

LOVER TYPES
Cynical / Spoiled / Rebellious / No Longer Looking / World-Weary

- If you assume an identity, the identity can also assume you.
- Sometimes it's easier to reveal the real you if you do it behind the pretense of being someone else. Role-playing can be freeing.
- "Fake it till you make it" may help some couples through periods of waning romance.

QUOTABLE

Claudette Colbert: You've got a name, haven't you?

Clark Gable: Yeah, I got a name. Peter Warne.

Claudette Colbert: Peter Warne. I don't like it.

Clark Gable: Don't let it bother you. You're giving it back to me in the morning.

Claudette Colbert: Pleased to meet you, Mr. Warne.

Clark Gable: The pleasure is all mine, Mrs. Warne.

THE STORY

Clark Gable and Claudette Colbert are at odds the second they lay eyes on each other. He's a reporter looking for a fresh scoop. She's a rich girl looking to marry an adventurer just to spite her controlling father. Clark promises to help her if she'll give him the exclusive on her story. They both think they know who the other one is and what they're all about. Along the way they get to know each other better and the walls between them begin to fall. However, it's when they pretend to be a married couple in order to stay in a roadside motel that things really begin to change. Ask actors how easy it is to fall in love with someone you're pretending to be in love with (we see this all the time in the celebrity gossip press). Playing man and wife for appearance's sake stirs up their emotions and by the end of the movie, they're headed that way in real life. There are times when pretending can make it so. Act as if you are freshly, intensely, eternally in love and it just might come to pass again. But stay away from the paparazzi.

TOOTSIE

RELEASE DATE
1982

BRIEF DESCRIPTION
Actor Dustin Hoffman dresses up as a woman to get more roles and develops a real friendship with Jessica Lange, whom he also is falling in love with. How can he become worthy of her as a man, while still pretending to be a woman?

CAST
Dustin Hoffman (Michael Dorsey / Dorothy Michaels / Tootsie), Jessica Lange (Julie)

LOVER TYPES
Insensitive / Prima Donna / Hesitant / Opening Up

DUSTIN HOFFMAN:
... I was a better man with you, as a woman... than I ever was with a woman, as a man.

- Walking a mile in the other person's high heels can produce a lot of understanding.
- Being on the receiving side of gender assumptions you've often made brings insight and hopefully the wisdom and courage to help change those assumptions and actions in others, too.
- Regardless of gender identity, romance and love are about self-respect and self-improvement for and because of the other person — and about giving them respect and kindness along with affection.

QUOTABLE

Dustin Hoffman: Look, you don't know me from Adam. But I was a better man with you, as a woman... than I ever was with a woman, as a man. You know what I mean? I just gotta learn to do it without the dress. At this point, there might be an advantage to my wearing pants. The hard part's over, you know? We were already... good friends.

THE STORY

Dustin Hoffman is a talented actor but very difficult to work with and he's just not getting parts anymore. What to do, what to do? He decides to disguise himself as a woman and go out for those roles and sure enough, he gets a great part in a TV soap. Complications arise because others believe he is a woman: some befriend her, like fellow actress Jessica Lange, and some fall for her, like Jessica's father. Meanwhile as a man he's having an affair with another actress. Talk about an identity crisis. At the end, though, he has had his epiphany and is a better person for it — whether as a man or a woman. This theme shows up in a lot of myths because there's a psychological advantage to "being" somebody different, particularly a different gender, in that we now have actual personal experience of another's realities. A bit of role-playing can result in understanding and empathy that can help us create ever so much kinder and responsive relationships.

SOME LIKE IT HOT

JACK LEMMON:
I'm a man!

JOE E. BROWN:
Well, nobody's perfect!

RELEASE DATE
1959

BRIEF DESCRIPTION
Musicians Tony Curtis and Jack Lemmon are on the lam from the mob, disguised as females in an all-girl band starring Marilyn Monroe. Mistaken identities confuse everyone as the guys try to stay alive while falling in love and fending off others' unwanted affections.

CAST
Marilyn Monroe (Sugar Kane Kowalczyk), Tony Curtis (Joe), Jack Lemmon (Jerry), Joe E. Brown (Osgood Fielding III)

LOVER TYPES
Naïve Romantic / Eternal Optimist / Competitive Playboy / The Sidekick

- The true quality of the heart shines through any disguise.
- It's in the kiss.
- Love doesn't care where you are on the gender spectrum.

QUOTABLE

Jack Lemon: I'm a man!

Joe E. Brown: Well, nobody's perfect!

THE STORY

Musicians Tony Curtis and Jack Lemmon are on the lam from the mob, disguised as females in an all-girl band. They both fall for the vocalist, Marilyn Monroe, and compete for her as best they can as women, which isn't very much. So Tony also fakes being an oil baron and woos Marilyn, who's taken by his shy charms. Jack, meanwhile, as a woman, has caught the eye of wealthy mamma's boy Joe E. Brown. The mobsters come to town, recognize Tony and Jack in spite of their disguises, and it's time to hit the road again. Tony tries to leave Marilyn behind and out of danger with a kind fib and a sweet kiss. She recognizes him from the kiss and jumps into the boat with him, Joe, and Jack. No matter what Tony says, Marilyn wants him. Now as for Joe: Jack keeps giving excuses why they can't marry and at the end reveals that he's not even a woman. Joe doesn't care — he fell for the person, not the gender. Something about true love sees through all our disguises and if we're smart we won't miss the boat on all that fun and joy.

CHAPTER 23

Worlds Apart

TWO WEEKS NOTICE

HUGH GRANT:

*When I say I'm poor,
I mean we may have
to share a helicopter
with another family.*

RELEASE DATE
2002

BRIEF DESCRIPTION

Developer Hugh Grant is filthy rich. Environmental attorney Sandra Bullock is definitely not. Her integrity and enthusiasm for her work start to win him over and he reaches across the dollar divide in hopes of gaining her approval by doing the right thing.

CAST

Hugh Grant (George Wade), Sandra Bullock (Lucy Kelson)

LOVER TYPES

Wealthy / Cavalier / Playboy / Business First / Middle-Class / Sincere / Altruistic / Strong / Honorable

- Love can change hearts more surely than politics or persuasion.
- Money comes and goes but love is a million times more precious.
- Dare to look past the surface and see not only who the person really is but who they might become.

QUOTABLE

Hugh Grant: I own the hotel, and I live there. My life is very much like Monopoly. I'm now poor. When I say I'm poor, I mean we may have to share a helicopter with another family.

THE STORY

Hugh Grant and Sandra Bullock are definitely worlds apart. He's a playboy billionaire developer. She's an environmental attorney. They come into conflict over an historical building she is trying to preserve and he is trying to tear down. Hugh hires her with a promise to save the building, then comes to admire and respect her for more than just her legal skills. She chafes under the demands of being not only his lawyer but his all-around advisor, including being called out of a wedding to help him decide what to wear. Sandra gives notice. Moved by her steadfast integrity as well as his undeniable attraction for her, Hugh has a change of heart. To hopefully win her back, he publicly apologizes and also announces he is indeed letting the community center remain, even at great financial loss. They are reunited, knowing both their lives will be quite different now that they're romantically together. Two things we see in this rom-com? You can often affect great change by going inside a system or a situation. And, it can be very freeing to realize you care for someone not *in spite* of who they are, but *because of* who they are.

ROMAN HOLIDAY

RELEASE DATE

1953

BRIEF DESCRIPTION

Audrey Hepburn is a royal princess looking for some duty-free fun, and Gregory Peck is a journalist looking for a story. They have a wonderful, adventurous time together and fall for each other romantically. But how long can their different worlds stay in the same orbit?

CAST

Audrey Hepburn (Princess Ann), Gregory Peck (Joe Bradley)

LOVER TYPES

Royalty / Naïve / Sweet / Over-Protected / Desirous of Change / Independent Professional / Worldly / Hidden Agenda / Street-Smart / Integrity

AUDREY HEPBURN:
I could do some of the things I've always wanted to.

GREGORY PECK:
Like what?

- When torn between duty and desire, assess how many people would be helped or harmed by which choice and let that help you decide.
- Sometimes the differences are just too much to overcome; but you can part graciously.
- You never know what's going to happen, so treasure each time together as if it were the last.

QUOTABLE

Audrey Hepburn: I could do some of the things I've always wanted to.

Gregory Peck: Like what?

Audrey Hepburn: Oh, you can't imagine. I'd do just whatever I liked all day long. Have fun. Maybe some excitement.

THE STORY

Caught between duty and desire, Princess Audrey Hepburn runs away from her stifling official agenda and spends marvelously freeing time exploring Rome with American reporter Gregory Peck, who's only too willing to squire her around in hopes of a news scoop. They fall for each other but the gap between the royal and the commoner is too vast. She must return to being the princess. He also does the noble thing and does not publish the photos or the story of her time being just a regular person. He becomes what in the beginning of the movie she desires when saying, "What the world needs is a return to sweetness and decency in the souls of its young men." Sometimes we must defer to duty and let desire fall out on the side of sweetness and decency. Not an easy thing to do, but truly, the world now more than ever really needs it.

MAID IN MAN-HATTAN

JENNIFER LOPEZ:
If I could rewind the past week, I would.

RALPH FIENNES:
Was any of it real?

RELEASE DATE
2002

BRIEF DESCRIPTION
Mistaken for a rich girl, hotel maid Jennifer Lopez lets wealthy politician Ralph Fiennes assume that it's true and enjoys time in his world of glamour and power. They're seriously falling for each other until the truth comes out.

CAST
Ralph Fiennes (Christopher Marshall), Jennifer Lopez (Marisa Ventura)

LOVER TYPES
Ambitious / Kind / Caring Parent / Dreamer / Altruistic / Concerned About Appearances

- Allow people, including yourself, to try out other worlds and other situations.
- Combining opposites can create a dynamic new union able to see different sides of many things.
- Think of your attraction to a different world as your future reaching out to pull you into it.

QUOTABLE

Jennifer Lopez: There was a part of me that wanted to know what it felt like, to have someone like you look at me the way you did just once. And I'm sorry. Truly. If I could rewind the past week, I would.

Ralph Fiennes: Was any of it real?

Jennifer Lopez: Yeah, it was real. It was so real I wondered how I was ever gonna give you up. But I had to give you up. That was the plan. And then, last night, I couldn't.

THE STORY

Jennifer Lopez is a single mom working as a hotel maid, hoping to move into management. Ralph Fiennes is a wealthy politician. Jennifer has tried on a guest's expensive coat when her young son asks if they can go for a walk with his new pal, Ralph. Ralph and Jennifer have instant sparks but she must hide that she's from a vastly different world. However, not before she dresses up and attends a ball with him. And spends a glorious night with him. Thrust across the divide between them by a quirk of timing, Jennifer stays there long enough to know it's about Ralph, not about position or money. Once found out, Jennifer is fired and she and Ralph separate but yearn for each other. Her son eventually reunites them and we see their successful pairing, her new career, and everybody happy. Curious enough to step into another world for a while? You might find it suits you just fine. Daring enough to look at someone without confining them to where-they-are-now? Giving others and ourselves permission to be and become whatever we desire can find differences falling away and the two worlds becoming one.

SABRINA

FATHERT:
... you're still reaching for the moon.

AUDREY HEPBURN:
No, Father. The moon's reaching for me!

RELEASE DATE
1954

BRIEF DESCRIPTION
Chauffeur's daughter Audrey Hepburn has always been infatuated with the younger son of the rich family her dad works for. Against his warnings not to overreach her station in life, Audrey — fresh from time in Paris — swirls headily into a romantic relationship with the older brother.

CAST
Humphrey Bogart (Linus Larrabee), Audrey Hepburn (Sabrina Fairchild)

LOVER TYPES
Confined by Convention / Hesitant About Love /

Responsible / Confident / Exuberant /
In Love with Life

- Love can build a bridge across gaps of class, age, wealth, position, culture...
- Try not to be intimidated by what seems like an insurmountable height — or depth — of difference between you because at the core it's only about who you really are.
- Think how very rich your combined experiences in different worlds can be.

QUOTABLE

Father: He's still David Larrabee, and you're still the chauffeur's daughter, and you're still reaching for the moon.
Audrey Hepburn: No, Father. The moon's reaching for *me*!

THE STORY

Audrey Hepburn lives on the other side of a huge divide of class and money. She's the daughter of the chauffeur of a very wealthy family but has a life-long crush on the wild-child younger son. After a stint in Paris she returns as a sophisticated young woman determined to be with him. Tasked with charming her away from his younger brother because she is, well, the chauffeur's daughter, confirmed bachelor Humphrey Bogart takes a turn at Sabrina. It works all too well and they find themselves falling for each other despite the gaps of age and social class. It seems love knows no boundaries, and if we're smart and want true happiness, we'll ignore them too.

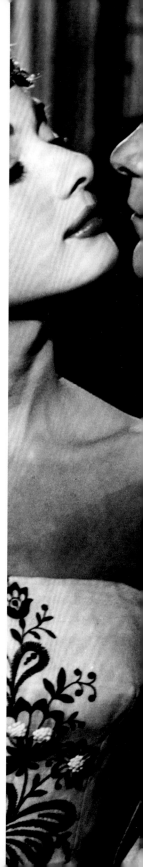

CHAPTER 24

Oops... Too Late? Did You Totally Miss This Opportunity?

FOUR WED- DINGS AND A FUNERAL

ANDIE MACDOWELL:
Just before I go, when were you thinking of announcing the engagement?

RELEASE DATE
1994

BRIEF DESCRIPTION
Always single Hugh Grant and new lover, Andie MacDowell, share a passionate encounter, then separate. Both seem to know they're missing something by not following up but neither does anything about it... until later.

CAST
Hugh Grant (Charles), Andie MacDowell (Carrie)

LOVER TYPES
Hesitant / Always the Bachelor / Confident / Surprised by Passion

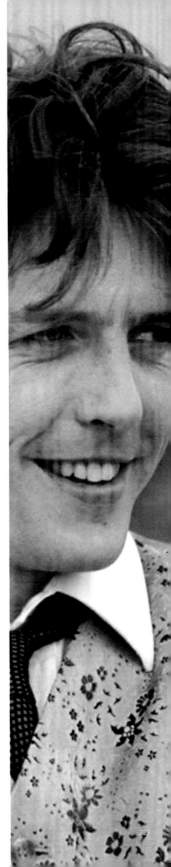

- Pay attention to those really strong feelings of attraction — they're really important.
- Things change. Don't settle for someone you don't really want or you may not be available when the person you do want is available again.
- If you feel a tugging, yearning pull when separating from a romantic encounter, look again to be sure it isn't your big chance slipping away.

QUOTABLE

Andie MacDowell: Just before I go, when were you thinking of announcing the engagement?

Hugh Grant: Uhh... I'm sorry, whose engagement?

Andie MacDowell: Ours. I assumed, since we slept together, that we would be getting married. What did you think?

Hugh Grant: What? I'm... gosh, you know, that's, umm... It takes a lot of thinking, that kind of thing, I mean, uhh... Obviously, I'm — You're joking! God, for a moment there, I thought I was in *Fatal Attraction*. I thought you were Glenn Close, and I was going to get home and find my pet rabbit in the stove.

Andie MacDowell: No... But I think we both missed a great opportunity here.

THE STORY

Hugh Grant is always going to weddings but always avoiding romantic entanglements in his own life. He's not sure why that is... maybe he just hasn't met the right girl or maybe it's just his avoidance of commitment. Then he meets Andie MacDowell and they're instantly attracted to each other. After making love she teases him about getting married but correctly intuits his avoidance issues. She goes on to marry someone else and he goes to more weddings and then a funeral, where he's struck by the love his friends share and that he has never experienced. He knows he lost the opportunity with Andie and is about to marry someone else when Andie comes back on the scene, now separated. Hugh is a lucky guy: He's dropped his own barriers and the one he really loves is available again. This time they won't let each other get away. In our own lives, time passes and things change. The trick is not to compromise when it comes to love because if you do, then you might not be available if and when real love reenters the picture. Or you might have to hurt a number of other people to finally be with that real love. Figure it out early, save other people's feelings by not leading them on, and enjoy more joy for a longer period of time.

MY BEST FRIEND'S WEDDING

RELEASE DATE
1997

BRIEF DESCRIPTION

Julia Roberts figured her backup groom Dermot Mulroney would always be available. Then when suddenly he's not, she's terrified she's lost her only opportunity for real love. Her funny but failed attempts to grasp him back may well give her some insights into who she is and what's really best for all.

JULIA ROBERTS:

Michael, I love you. I've loved you for nine years.

CAST

Julia Roberts (Julianne Potter), Dermot Mulroney (Michael O'Neal), Rupert Everett (George Downes), Cameron Diaz (Kimberly Wallace)

LOVER TYPES

Self-Centered / Panicked / Possessive / Win-at-All-Costs / Sure / Kind but Deflecting

- Sometimes you've already lost something and you just need to be realistic and realize that ship has sailed, that soufflé has fallen, that game is over, that opportunity is gone. And that that's okay.
- Take a good look at what didn't work and why so you'll at least not make that particular mistake again.
- Maybe what looks like a lost opportunity in love is really a found opportunity to learn more about yourself.

QUOTABLE

Julia Roberts: Michael, I love you. I've loved you for nine years. I've just been too arrogant and scared to realize it, and, well, now, I'm just scared, so — I realize this comes at a very inopportune time, but I really have this gigantic favor to ask of you. Choose me. Marry me. Let me make you happy. Oh, that sounds like three favors, doesn't it? But...

THE STORY

Julia Roberts figured her long-time best friend and former lover, Dermot Mulroney, would always be available to fulfill their pledge that if they're not married to others by a certain age they'll marry each other. They've gone their separate ways for a while and she suddenly learns he's about to be married. Her fallback love option is going away! Julia is a woman on a mission to sabotage that wedding and win back Dermot. Desperate times call for desperate measures but she does some pretty despicable things along the way to realizing she actually does like his fiancée, Cameron Diaz. With the help of her friend Rupert Everett, Julia realizes she has already really lost Dermot in that way and needs to accept it, let them go, and start dancing! We need to discern between something we really want and something we are just hanging on to so we needn't be alone. It can make all the difference in a happy or an unfulfilled romantic life. And it can't hurt to do some dancing, either.

LOVE ACTUALLY

RELEASE DATE

2003

BRIEF DESCRIPTION

Andrew Lincoln's in love with his best friend's bride, Keira Knightly. He doesn't want to break up their marriage but he does want her to know how he feels. The way he does it is honorable, charming, and sweet. His wisdom is rewarded.

CAST

Keira Knightly (Juliet), Andrew Lincoln (Mark)

LOVER TYPES

New Bride / Confident / Content / Unrequited Lover / Shy / Loyal to Friendship

ANDREW LINCOLN:
... at Christmas you tell the truth — to me you are perfect...

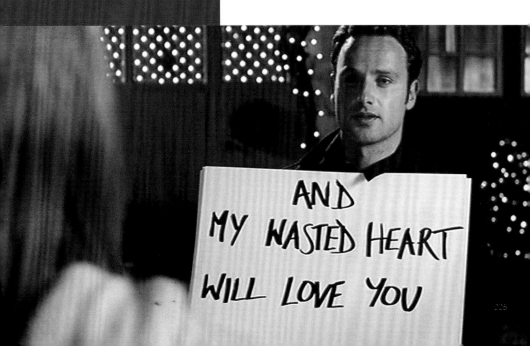

AND MY WASTED HEART WILL LOVE YOU

- Take the higher ground in your expression of romantic love and you'll win honor and respect.
- Love is a battlefield, so it's said. It's also like a game. Some win, some do not. Be a good sport about losing and you'll actually be a winner.
- Done well and sensitively, acknowledging feelings you won't be acting on can be positive and nonthreatening. Doing that can build trust and really enhance friendships.

QUOTABLE

Andrew Lincoln: For now let me say, without hope or agenda, just because it's Christmas — and at Christmas you tell the truth — to me you are perfect and my wasted heart will love you until you look like this.... Merry Christmas.

THE STORY

Andrew Lincoln's best friend has just married Keira Knightly. Mutual friends think Andrew's reticence toward the bride is because he's in love with the groom or that he just doesn't like her. Yet when watching the wedding video he took, Keira sees most of it is focused on her. Andrew reluctantly confesses that it's self-preservation: He actually does love her but would never do anything to mess up the marriage or the friendships. Then on Christmas Eve he comes by with Christmas carols on a boom box and a declaration about his missed opportunity on cue cards. It's a charming, heartfelt, chivalrous encounter and Keira rewards him with a warm, appreciative, friendly kiss that preserves his dignity. Yes, he lost this one, but he was courageous enough to express his love, and as he says to himself as he walks away, "Enough. Enough for now." Unexpressed love can gnaw at us and neither pining away nor stalking are healthy options. A heartfelt agenda-less declaration like Andrew's can clear the air and free all parties to move on with respect.

SLEEP-LESS IN SEATTLE

MEG RYAN:

What do you think — ?

RELEASE DATE
1993

BRIEF DESCRIPTION

Meg Ryan has really fallen for Tom Hanks's voice and poignant story over the radio, even though she's engaged to a nice-enough guy. Torn by her emotions and fearful she'll miss her chance at true love, she asks her therapist brother for advice. Will she find the courage to follow her desires?

CAST

Meg Ryan (Annie Reed), David Hyde Pierce (Dennis Reed), Tom Hanks (Sam Baldwin)

LOVER TYPES

Confused / Unsure About What or Who They Really Want / Hesitant / Analytical / Brotherly / Supportive

LOVE LESSONS

- Seek advice from those who know you well.
- Seek advice from relationship specialists. If they're one and the same, lucky you.
- You'll probably regret the things you didn't do more than the things you did do. Be brave and reach out.

QUOTABLE

Meg Ryan: But what I really don't want to do is end up always wondering what might have happened and knowing I could have done something. What do you think — ?

THE STORY

Meg Ryan confesses to her therapist brother that she's afraid if she doesn't follow up on her feelings for Tom Hanks she may regret it. They haven't even met but she's intrigued by his voice and story. Tom's a widower and his young son wants a new mom, so he gets him on a radio show talking about how he misses his wife, what he loved about her, why he hasn't moved on. Meg is struck by his sincerity... and something else. Her growing feelings for this man she's never met trouble her, in part because she's already engaged to a nice enough guy. She invites Tom to meet at the Empire State Building like in the movie *An Affair to Remember* but doesn't send the letter. A friend of hers does and then Tom's son is instrumental in getting them together. Meg has broken off her engagement, Tom has taken a giant step toward new love, and their first meeting is all the magic all three of them hoped it would be. If you have a feeling you might miss a marvelous opportunity with someone, at least take a step or two in that direction. If it doesn't work, you'll have no regrets. If it does, you too may find the magic.

CHAPTER 25

Finding Love Where You Least Expect It

MOON-STRUCK

NICOLAS CAGE:

... love don't make things nice — it ruins everything.

RELEASE DATE

1987

BRIEF DESCRIPTION

As Cher discovers to her great dismay, real love is closer to home than she thought — in her soon-to-be brother-in-law Nicolas Cage. Their intense attraction throws everything around them into chaos and both must decide how to handle this irresistible passion.

CAST

Cher (Loretta Castorini), Nicolas Cage (Ronny Cammareri)

LOVER TYPES

Loner / Rebellious / Reluctant / Irresistible / Romantic / Possessed by Passion

- Your destined love may not be over the horizon — they could be right there in front of you.
- Love changes everything so expect a whole lot of changes when you find it.
- Never shut down your antennae for love, but once you're really there you won't even be interested in anyone else.

QUOTABLE

Nicolas Cage: Loretta, I love you. Not like they told you love is, and I didn't know this either, but love don't make things nice — it ruins everything. It breaks your heart. It makes things a mess. We aren't here to make things perfect. The snowflakes are perfect. The stars are perfect. Not us. Not us! We are here to ruin ourselves and to break our hearts and love the wrong people and die. The storybooks are bullshit. Now I want you to come upstairs with me and get in my bed!

THE STORY

Cher is engaged to a very nice man whom she's not in love with. She meets his estranged brother, Nicolas Cage, and the sparks fly and all her plans go awry when they fall irresistibly into each other's arms. She tries to walk away from this unexpected love, but a full moon, a night at the opera, and lovemaking afterward bring them even closer. Though insecurities and infidelities abound in her family, Cher's daring to embrace love seems to inspire the others, and when the first brother breaks their engagement, Nicolas grabs up the ring and proposes to Cher. She accepts and all the family signs on to the new situation. Sometimes that unexpected place is right in front of our eyes, within our inner circle. When looking for love we need nearsightedness as well as farsightedness lest we overlook the opportunity for real passion.

LEAP YEAR

MATTHEW GOODE:
Have a little faith that it will all work out.

RELEASE DATE
2010

BRIEF DESCRIPTION

On a mission to propose to her boyfriend, Amy Adams encounters cynical Irishman Matthew Goode and hires him to help her. As barriers continue to pop up along the way, she's thrown into his arms and starts to open her mind and her heart.

CAST

Amy Adams (Anna), Matthew Goode (Declan)

LOVER TYPES

Focused / Professionally Successful / Big City / Control Freak / Country / Cynical / Laid-Back

LOVE LESSONS

- People with plans can become prisoners to those plans.

- That attractive, troubling stranger who just came into your life? They might just be the love of your life.
- Pay attention to what that other person really values because that really matters.

Matthew Goode: Here's an idea. Why don't you stop trying to control everything in the known universe. ... Have a little faith that it will all work out.

THE STORY

Amy Adams, rather a control freak, is following her boyfriend to Dublin to propose on Leap Day. Once in Ireland weather glitches throw her plans into disarray and she ends up at a small-town inn owned by gruff and cynical Matthew Goode. She hires him to drive her to Dublin but they're thwarted by herds of cattle, a tour of castle ruins, sudden rain, and a missed train. At a local B&B they must pose as married to be accepted as guests by the conservative owners. The pose includes a romantic kiss, the magic of which takes them both by surprise. Finally in Dublin, Amy proposes to her boyfriend, he accepts, and they return to America. But when she learns he accepted mainly so they'd be approved for a condo sale, she leaves and goes back to Ireland. Amy proposes to Matthew that they "not make plans together." He counter-proposes that they do make plans together. And they do. Too often we have a fixed scenario of how our romantic relationships must go and we close our eyes to finding love in unexpected places. For a possibly very pleasant surprise, try letting go of control and be open to what might happen.

THE WEDDING DATE

DERMOT MULRONEY:
I think I'd miss you even if we'd never met.

RELEASE DATE
2005

BRIEF DESCRIPTION
Still wounded from a breakup, Debra Messing hires Dermot Mulroney to be her date for a wedding. They find themselves quite attracted to each other and struggling to sort out who's what, where, and why.

CAST
Dermot Mulroney (Nick Mercer), Debra Messing (Kat Ellis)

LOVER TYPES
Wounded / Image-Conscious / Professional Escort / Observant / Sensitive

- Don't rule someone out based on what they do or why you're interacting with them.
- Sometimes the substitute becomes the real thing.
- There's something about "acting as if" that can free up our deeper feelings.

QUOTABLE

Dermot Mulroney: I think I'd miss you even if we'd never met.

THE STORY

Debra Messing hires professional escort Dermot Mulroney as her date for a wedding to make her ex-fiancé jealous and show her family she's not a lonely spinster. What starts out as a business arrangement with no interpersonal agenda evolves into a recognition of strong attraction. Confessions of affairs abound and people are breaking up all over the place. Debra offends Dermot when she pays him for sex and he departs, leaving the money behind. But he meets up with the troubled groom and convinces him that love in the right-now is more important than mistakes in the past. Taking his own advice, he also returns, the wedding takes place, and Debra and Dermot get together. Two pieces of advice clash here at first: "Don't date the help," and "Act as if." She unexpectedly hired exactly the right man to pose as her boyfriend and the posing became reality. We might find love in the person of someone we cast in the role of beloved, even if at first it's just in our imagination.

THE APRIL FOOLS

CATHERINE DENEUVE:
No, tonight we only say what we really mean.

RELEASE DATE
1969

BRIEF DESCRIPTION

Businessman Jack Lemmon and his boss's trophy wife, Catherine Deneuve, meet at a party and, without knowing who each other is, find themselves greatly attracted. She's headed back to Paris and they decide he should go with her. Can he make the break from his regular life?

CAST

Jack Lemmon (Howard Brubaker), Catherine Deneuve (Catherine Gunther)

LOVER TYPES

Unhappily Married / Unfulfilled Professionally / Trophy Wife /

Yearning for Love / Desperate to be Real / Daring to Break Conventions

- Dare to break out of the confines of your cultural norms.
- When someone treats you better than others treat you, pay attention.
- If you're wanting a change, be brave enough to take the steps to make a change.

QUOTABLE

Jack Lemmon: I was going to say something I thought I should say, but I didn't mean it.
Catherine Deneuve: No, tonight we only say what we really mean.
Jack Lemmon: And do what we really want to do.

THE STORY

Jack Lemmon never expected to find love anywhere. His self-absorbed wife rarely listens to him at all. His life as a businessman is just like all the others — full of shallow, meaningless duties. Catherine Deneuve is a trophy wife in a hollow marriage; the initial attraction has faded and she's about to walk away from it all. They meet and suddenly find something unexpected in each other. He finds a kind, sensitive woman who appreciates his own decency and sensitivity and who actually listens to him with interest. She finds a man who sees more than her external beauty and who actually listens to her. As he says, she's a princess and he's a frog who because of her kiss is now a prince. She's heading back to Paris and he decides to cross the boundaries of the expected and go with her. They are both excited and scared to be taking this giant leap together. But when where you are isn't where you want to be, be open to the unexpected.

About the Author

PAMELA JAYE SMITH is a mythologist, author, international consultant-speaker, and award-winning writer-producer-director with over thirty years' experience in the media industry, in Hollywood and around the world.

Credits include Fox, Disney, Paramount, Microsoft, Universal, RAI-TV Rome, Romance Writers of America, UCLA, USC Film School, American Film Institute, Women in Film, Natl. Film Institute of Denmark, LA and Marseille WebFests, and many film festivals and story conferences. Others are American Assoc. of University Women, Junior ROTC, GM, Boeing, Hyundai, Hughes Space & Comm., the FBI, and the US Army.

Ms. Smith has served on various think tanks: the US Army's Advanced Warfighting Working Group at Fort Knox giving presentations on the Warrior Archetype; the Entertainment Industries Council promoting The Art of Making a Difference; and Boeing's Workforce Development group promoting science, technology, engineering, and math to young people. She is on the Board of Advisors for the LAWeb Fest, the Center for Conscious Creativity, and the Orpheus Project.

Pamela is the founder of MYTHWORKS, cofounder of Alpha Babe Academy, and cofounder of Mythic Challenges: Create Stories that Change the World.

www.mythworks.net
www.alphababeacademy.com
www.mythicchallenges.com